Dear
Siena, Tobler Will & Walter
and family
Be well the
Simple way
♡ Amy xoxo

Nourishment Made Simple Cookbook and Wellness Guide

Whole Food Recipes for Kids and the Busy Family

Amy Hudgens, B.A., CNC

Contributor:
JoEllen DeNicola, N.E

Foreword by:
Elizabeth Lipski, PhD, CCN, CNS, LDN

Busy Bee Nutrition

Nourishment Made Simple

ISBN-10: 153312048X
ISBN-13: 978-1533120489

Cover and Interior Design - Carina Sterzenbach

Illustrations - Debbie Merritt Bruflat

Photography - Jeanie Gartin and Amy Hudgens

Editors - Jennifer Freese, Carina Sterzenbach and Mike Hudgens

Second Edition Editor – Sarah Wilmarth

Dedication Page

I dedicate this book to:

My mom Sue Wheeler- My strong "warrior" mother and the funniest person! You will always be in my heart.

And of course... Mike, Nylah, my late grandma and grandpa Betty and Dan Foley.

Preface to the 2nd Edition

Welcome to the Second Edition of Nourishment Made Simple Cookbook and Wellness Guide!

My intention for creating this cookbook three years ago was to help and inspire busy families (and all busy people) t o be able to create nourishing foods in a quick and easy way. I constantly found myself wishing for a Simple guide with foods kids will enjoy that I could hand clients in my consulting practice. I finally decided to make one. This cookbook is also a grassroots project, simple and self-published. Needless to say, this amazing project was in need of some updating so that was my first inspiration for wanting to produce the second edition.

The Second Edition of Nourishment Made Simple Cookbook and Wellness Guide includes the following:

- 27 new and amazing simple recipes
- A Simple Index! Yes!
- Some added nutritional information
- Two new Wellness Pages for your enjoyment
- New simple resource guides for local and national practitioners

I hope my cookbook can be your "go to" guide for Simple and Nourishing foods for your busy family. It's a gift to me to be able to help people eat whole foods that are nutrient dense the *Simple WAY*. I am grateful to all of you who purchase a copy of my cookbook and cook with your family! Thank You.

With love,

Amy Hudgens, B.A., CNC

Table of Contents

Acknowledgements

I want to first thank my amazing husband Mike Hudgens for his patience and constant support with my many projects. I love and appreciate you lovey!

♥ ♥ ♥

Thanks to my daughter Nylah for inspiring me everyday. Mommy loves cooking with you AND that you eat all your veggies on your plate! You are my greatest gift.

♥ ♥ ♥

Thanks to my mother, Sue Wheeler for always feeding me healthy protein and veggies every night for dinner growing up. As a busy single mom, you always made sure we ate balanced! Thanks for your support and encouragement daily.

♥ ♥ ♥

Thanks to my Grandma, Betty for always being such a strong woman in my life. Thanks for always supporting me.

♥ ♥ ♥

Thanks to all my friends and family who are too many to mention for all your love and support.

♥ ♥ ♥

I give sincere thanks to my friend and contributor of this cookbook JoEllen DeNicola. You have been the best mentor I could ever imagine. I appreciate your support and guidance over the years. Thank you for believing in me. We did it!

♥ ♥ ♥

I give thanks to Elizabeth Lipski, PhD, CCN, CNS, LDN author of *Digestive Wellness for Children* for writing the foreword & for the healing books you have written. I am forever grateful.

♥ ♥ ♥

Thank you to Terry Walters author of *Clean Food* for writing a supportive comment. I love your books and use them often. It's an honor having you be part of this project.

♥ ♥ ♥

Thank you Dr. Sunjya Schweig, Functional Medical Doctor for all the amazing and healing work you do with patients and the community daily and for your support with this project.

♥ ♥ ♥

My deepest appreciation to my editors: Jennifer Freese, Carina Sterzenbach, and Sarah Wilmarth. Thank you for the many hours you worked on this cookbook. I am very grateful for you all.

♥ ♥ ♥

Thanks to Carina Sterzenbach for designing an amazing cover and back cover! You are so talented and creative.

♥ ♥ ♥

To Debbie Merritt Bruflat for providing the beautiful and hand drawn illustrations. My deepest thanks to you my doula and friend.

♥ ♥ ♥

Thanks to Jeanie Gartin for taking great pictures that I was able to use for my cookbook. I love and thank you.

♥ ♥ ♥

Thanks to Jessica Jacobsen, Erin Shea and JoEllen DeNicola for contributing educational and amazing wellness pages.

♥ ♥ ♥

To all the practitioners and business owners I reference in the local resource page, I am so grateful to work with you all and think you are the best at what you do.

♥ ♥ ♥

Thanks to my rock star editor of the second edition, Sarah Wilmarth, for all the blood, sweat, and tears you put in.

♥ ♥ ♥

To my friends that contributed recipes, I am so thankful for each and every nutrient-dense recipe you provided. Thanks for being part of this special project I believe in so much.

♥ ♥ ♥

With Love and Thanks,
Amy Hudgens

Eat A Rainbow On Your Plate
AND Make It FUN

Foreword

By Elizabeth Lipski, Ph.D., CCN, CNS, LDN

You are what you eat. So are your children. Each cell in their body is made from the fats, proteins, carbohydrates, vitamins, minerals, water, bacteria, yeasts, and phytonutrients that comprise our food. Providing nutrient dense meals and snacks is one of the most important things you can do to help set up your children for success later in life. According to the World Health Organization, providing a healthful diet for your children reduces cardiovascular disease, type II diabetes, obesity, mental health and depression. Good food during infancy and the early years determines your child's immune strength lifelong. Early nutrition can even help determine your ability to learn well, study easily and ultimately determines your ability to earn money in the work place.

Preparing family meals is critically important to your child's development and your family's health. According to the National Longitudinal Survey of Adolescent Health, children who participate in family meals are 24% more likely to eat healthier foods, 35% less likely to have an eating disorder, and have a 12% reduced risk of being obese. According to the *Journal of Adolescent Health*, eating together at least 4 times a week has great benefits that continue to improve if you eat together even more often. They report that your adolescent will experience better emotional and behavior health, feel a greater sense of well being, be more helpful, and have an increased sense of trust. Other studies report improved communication skills, higher self-esteem, increased motivation, and lower delinquency rates and drug usage. *Nourishment Made Simple: Cookbook and Wellness Guide* provides the recipes and tools to cook yummy family meals. Being a parent can be overwhelming. I remember the responsibility of taking care of my children and also providing them with nourishing meals. I wanted recipes and meal and snacks ideas that were fast, easy and that everyone in the family would eat! When I made something that met those criteria, I'd put it on a list I kept on the refrigerator. If I got the recipe from a cookbook, I'd write down the name of the book and the page number. After all, when it's 5 o'clock and you are the chief cook...it's great to have reminders so that you don't make the same 4 dishes over and over again. In *Nourishment Made Simple* you'll find tips for emergency dinners that can get you out of a jam!

Nourishment Made Simple provides you with a large variety of simple, nutrient dense, kid-tested recipes. Amy Hudgens has road tested these in her own home and by teaching the Rainbow Greens Nutrition program in a preschool. She's seen firsthand the delight of children when they can taste these foods.

You will find tips on improving the nutritional content of meals and snacks. Amy Hudgens provides tips and tricks and "cheat" sheets to help you maximize each bite. Broaden what you eat; improve the variety. Discover more ideas for quick box lunches. Make almond flour pancakes, blueberry granola, or pumpkin breakfast cookies for breakfast. What child wouldn't want to eat a Banana Almond Butter Boat or Red Ants on a Log? Making nori wraps with your children provides iodine for brain function and is also a fun family project! Amy also provides great dinner, salad, lunch, and smoothie recipes.

Nourishment Made Simple is a fantastic way to make each bite count and improve the health and well being of your entire family. I hope that this book becomes a dog-eared favorite. Enjoy!

Elizabeth Lipski, Ph.D., CCN, CNS, LDN
Academic Director of Nutrition & Integrative Health programs
Maryland University of Integrative Health
Author of *Digestive Wellness for Children*

Introduction

This cookbook and wellness guide was created to inspire *The Busy Family* to feel less stressed about preparing **Nourishing** and **Simple** meals and snacks on the go. When we are busy, we eat more processed foods and we often don't meal plan or eat enough whole foods. Being rushed, stressed and tired is a combination that most often leads to poor food choices. The typical story that we all know all to well goes like this, " its Monday 6 pm kids are hungry, tired and so are the parents and we have nothing **Healthy** to prepare and eat **QUICK**". Sound familiar? It sure does to me! Being busy and stressed is when we should be nourishing our body the most!

Nourishment Made Simple Cookbook and Wellness Guide, gives you the tools to be able to fuel your body and mind with whole foods recipes that are simple to prepare. It's so much easier to plan, prep and cook nourishing foods when we have simple recipes and guides to help lead the way and take the stress off.

As a Nutrition teacher at local preschools, I see how important it is to make sure our kids are being nourished all day long. This cookbook and wellness guide provides lots of simple and unprocessed lunch box recipes that kids will love.

This is the perfect cookbook for the whole family and I hope you enjoy exploring the recipes and guides inside.

A Note from the Author

My greatest inspiration for writing this cookbook and wellness guide comes from my deep desire to prepare nourishing and nutrient-dense foods for my daughter Nylah and my family that are SIMPLE to prepare. I am a busy mom, wife and business owner, I needed to figure out how I could nourish myself, my family and help support my clients in a SIMPLE way. This is when I started the process of creating *Nourishment Made Simple Cookbook and Wellness Guide*.

I have been dreaming of writing this cookbook for over 3 years. At the time, I was a new, busy and VERY tired mom that wanted to eat nourishing foods that were simple to prepare but could not figure out how to balance it all. I had just started my nutrition business, had a one-year-old child and was overwhelmed. I was having many discussions with other new moms that were feeling the same way. I knew in my heart and soul that I had to create a cookbook that could help support busy families feel less stressed, nourished and have more energy the SIMPLE way.

I reached out to JoEllen DeNicola, my mentor and also the contributor to this cookbook and asked for her help on my cookbook project. It's been 3 busy years of talking about the vision and gathering information along the way. Finally, this year was the time to put it all together and make it happen.

Nourishment Made Simple Cookbook and Wellness Guide, focuses on whole foods recipes that are nutrient-dense, unprocessed, kid friendly and delicious. I wanted to create a cookbook that many people can enjoy with a variety of different diets. Almost all the recipes are gluten-free. All of the recipes are created with love. I hope to inspire you all to cook some of these recipes with your kids and families.

Thanks so much for supporting my dream!

Much Love,

Amy Hudgens - Author
Busybeenutrition.com

A Note from the Contributor
JoEllen DeNicola, N.E

Food is the foundation of health, and it is more. It is the portal to reconnecting with the Earth that supports us, the community that cares for us, our cultural and our familial roots. Through flavors, textures, smells, and tastes we bring the world of plants and animals into ourselves. They in fact become us.

So what better way to acquaint ourselves and our family with the Earth, Sun, Water, Air and Ethers that contain all of us than to serve them in the form of whole food meals? Knowing that you are eating a simple yet tasty nutritious, delicious dinner from freshly grown whole foods and feeling, tasting, experiencing the difference they make in your family's lives, that is essential to well being and to good health.

May you find that your family's health grows strong and vital; and may you understand that you and the plants of the Earth are truly relatives.

Many Blessings,
JoEllen DeNicola

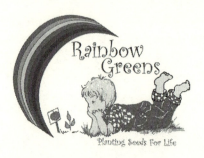

Rainbow Greens Nutrition Program For Kids
Planting Seeds For Life

I created Rainbow Greens Nutrition Program in May of 2012. The program started as a Pilot Program with a 4-month trial period at a local preschool called Mixed Greens in Santa Rosa, CA. I teach preschoolers about nutrition through fun games, cooking together, being in the garden and much more. The children at Mixed Greens are very interactive during our once a month lesson and have so much fun.

After the 4-month trial went well, Mixed Greens Preschool decided to make Rainbow Greens Nutrition Program part of their curriculum. Every month when I would start teaching, the children would say "Miss Amy I have been eating my greens" AND "Miss Amy I have been eating a rainbow on my plate". This was progress in my eyes and I am so proud of the kids. It is so fulfilling and inspiring to me to teach young children about where there food is grown, where it comes from and why it is good for us, while getting them excited about trying new foods and cooking with their families.

With Love and Thanks,
Amy Hudgens, CNC – Busy Bee Nutrition
Founder of Rainbow Greens

Rainbow Greens in Action

Food can be fun!

Chapter 1: Wellness Guide

Nourishing Kids One School Lunch at a Time
Jessica Jacobsen, Chef

nour·ish·ing
'nəriSHiNG/
adjective
adjective: **nourishing**
   1   (of food) containing substances necessary for growth,
        health, and good condition.

My passion for food started very young. As an infant, I was hospitalized for a dangerously high fever, which almost cost me my life. My mother swore her Puerto Rican version of a "smoothie" which she bottle fed me at the hospital, cured her sickly baby: yautia, platano, guineo, mango, leche and a hefty amount of calories. From that moment on, insofar as my mom was responsible for me, she would never stop trying to plump me up. It worked. By the third grade, I weighed 100 pounds and this shy, chubby, half Puerto Rican girl was the butt of many jokes. My mother was an amazing cook and although her attempt to keep me healthy by encouraging obesity was ill advised, it inspired a lifelong love of food. Additionally, being overweight as a child has motivated me in my adult life to develop a deep understanding of diet and nutrition especially as it relates to children.

I have been cooking for as long as I can remember but it wasn't until I had my son, and was in the midst of working in the career I had chosen, that I decided to start a catering company. I wanted the flexibility to care for my baby and I felt a sudden calling to cook professionally. Soon thereafter, I started making lunches for my first school; Ma Petite E'cole; a little French preschool in Santa Rosa.

My endless preaching about encouraging young children to eat wholesome grown-up food was suddenly being supported by the French philosophy on childrearing. The first day at Ma

20

Petite E'cole, I served lamb with roasted potatoes. Needless to say, the staff cheered. Those little guys loved it and I was inspired. "Food immersion" works on the same principle as language immersion by surrounding children with a culture of healthy eating. Therefore, the school setting, with its heavy peer influence, presents the perfect environment for supporting young children in developing healthy eating habits. And this investment will inevitably have a positive effect on their palettes and the choices they make later in life.

In the years that I worked at Ma Petite E'cole and later at the Santa Rosa French American Charter, I saw kids eat dishes that I never thought imaginable: ground pork with olives and capers, chicken with prunes and black rice. Parents feared that their kids, the pickiest of eaters, wouldn't try new things. I realized that as a culture we have dumbed down food for our children. In both lunch programs, we used gentle encouragement, an enjoyable eating experience, and colorful food combinations that were visually appealing, bold and yet simple. The results: even the finickiest of eaters became more adventurous. Although it was an investment in time and energy, the results were notable.

The issue with the way kids are fed, particularly in the school system, isn't only about the food, which is obviously a big problem. The connections that are made through food are lost when eating ceases to be an experience. Being nourished engages many aspects of our well being: social, physical, and emotional. When I started the school lunch service company, Pharm: Food for Thought (pharmfoodforthought.com) with my business partner, Nutritionist, Jennifer Foege, we knew we wanted to set ourselves apart. Not only do we provide an amazing buffet style, made from scratch lunch, but also something personal for the children and their parents. Using my experience at Ma Petite E'cole and the French American Charter along with Jennifer's expertise on diet and nutrition, we have created what we hope will serve as model for school districts.

Being fueled by nourishing food creates a foundation for mental acuity and can also be a vehicle for learning. School districts may hold the key to shifting the growing health crisis by redirecting their resources to emphasize healthy eating. Despite overwhelming evidence that this shift would have an enormous impact on our children, school districts remain resistant to change. The pressure must come from us; parents, educators and people who care about the health of our future generations.

Jessica Jacobsen

The Healthy Lunch Box
By Amy Hudgens, B.A, CNC

Eating a nourishing breakfast is the first step to be able to help start the day feeling balanced, nourished and supported nutritionally. Eating healthy snacks and lunch at school can help support your children throughout the day in a Healthy Way!

Why should your child's lunch box be healthy?
- Helps to improve your child's behavior
- Supports more stable blood sugar
- Helps with improved attention span
- Supports overall better mood
- Teaches your child that nutrient-dense foods can be yummy too!

Important Daily Lunch Box Items:
- Protein-provided energy and stable blood sugar
- Fats-supports brain health and mood
- Unrefined carbohydrates- provides needed energy
- No refined sugar and limited fruit
- Clean Water - proper hydration all day is key! If we are dehydrated we are tired!

Some examples of Nourishing Foods for "the healthy lunch box"- Dinner left overs are great for next day school lunches, so make EXTRA dinner!
- Cooked chopped organic chicken
- Avocado slices
- Pumpkin seeds
- Nut butters
- Organic yogurt
- Chopped Colorful Veggies
- Cut up Colorful Fruits
- Nourishing soups
- Organic applesauce

- Grass Fed Beef cut into small pieces

Tip: If there is a NO nut policy at your school due to allergies, see if you can bring a "seed" butter. Use sunflower seed butter instead!

My Favorite Lunch Boxes and Insulated Food Jars for School Lunch:

- *LunchBots Duo Stainless Steel food container – Amazon.com*
- *Crocodile Creek Insulated Food Jar - Amazon.com*
- *Mason Jars are always great, depending on school policy and child's age*

Why Visiting Farms With Your Kids Is SO Important
By Erin Shea – Former Farm Owner

As a mother of two young children, and former director of a non-profit that aims to connect children with where their food comes from and get them excited about growing food sustainably and eating well, I think exposing children to gardens and farms is essential.

When kids would come to our farm, they try things they would never try for their parents, and they are often jumping at the chance to do so! By getting them out of their usual environment, teaching them about the process of growing food, and allowing them to physically connect with that process, they learn that growing and eating healthy foods can be fun! And once they've tried something new, they feel a sense of empowerment and want to share it with others.

We recently had a group of students from San Francisco come to our farm. Most of them had never been to a farm, and when asked what kinds of vegetables they liked to eat, the list was quite short. We walked around the farm, talking about what was growing and how we cared for them. Before I knew it, the kids who were reluctant to try anything, were gulping down fresh veggie juice and begging to pick more kale for a raw kale salad! They went home excited to share their experience with their family, ready to bring some of the new foods they tried into their regular diets, and also understanding the importance of growing our food in a way that doesn't harm ourselves or the environment.

My own kids can sometimes make eating veggies a challenge, but when I remind them that the cucumbers are the ones they picked, suddenly it's fun to eat them and not a chore. They even brag to their friends at school that they helped grow the veggies in their lunch.

Fun at the farm with the family

Boosting Immunity Made Simple!

There are so many things you can do to boost your immunity! I am going to share with you some of my little shortcuts on how to stay Nourished and Boosted all year long.

The Basics:

- Pick one new "bulk" item each week from the bins at grocery store. Fun!
- Healthy diet filled with lots of whole foods. Eat a rainbow on your plate!
- Eat foods in season. Eat warming foods - roasted veggies, soups and stews.
- Hand washing - teach your children to wash their hands a lot. Sing the ABC's.
- Good sleep for both kiddos and parents
- Exercise daily and laugh a lot
- Stress management and lots of love
- Reduce or cut out refined sugar

Inflammation and our Gut:

Approximately 70% of our immunity lives in our digestive tract. So when illness strikes take a closer look at the gut. Chronic inflammation can lead to illness.

- Eat more alkaline forming foods to help boost immunity. It's all about balance! Taking daily probiotics to help protect the gut is a great idea for kids and adults.
- Increase your daily intake of fermented foods.
- Take a good Omega-3 daily supplement - can help with inflammation.
- Do you have enough HCL (stomach acid) and enzymes in your gut? This is stomach acid balance.
- Slippery elm, DGL, aloe and l-glutamine may help with soothing inflammation.

Nourishing foods to boost immunity:
- Rainbow on the plate!
- Eat food with few ingredients
- Eat protein & healthy fats
- Fermented foods - miso, kefir, and sauerkraut (gut friendly & healthy bacteria)
- Enjoy some sea veggies - kombu, arami and nori
- Mushrooms - mushrooms can help build immunity
- Nourishing teas and broths
- Oats - relaxes the nerves, reduces cholesterol, and have lots of fiber

When illness strikes: Visit Farmacopia Integrative Pharmacy in Santa Rosa for nourishing wellness tinctures and supplements OR go to your local health food store.

Emergency Foods Made Simple!
Have dinner ready in 10 minutes

I talk a lot to my nutrition clients and families about stocking up on "emergency foods" for an ***extra quick dinner***. These foods are meant to be for "emergency purposes" and not eaten everyday. I encourage you to meal plan and prep weekly to make your week less stressful when it comes to cooking dinner. However, we all have those days where 6pm came all too fast and we need a meal on the table super fast...here are some emergency food options:

Keep in freezer:
Garden burgers
Frozen turkey or veggie meatballs
Beans that you made from scratch
Pasta sauce
Pesto

Keep on hand:
BPA-free canned beans
Tuna in a packet – try to buy line-caught
Red sauce in a jar

Keep in fridge:
Cooked Chicken – quick chicken salad
Washed mixed salad greens
Turkey Bacon - Make a BLTA sandwich - see recipe my recipe on page 89.

Side note:
I realize that these foods have lots of extra sodium and are not the freshest foods SO only use them on an emergency basis! We want to focus on fresh, clean, organic and nutrient dense foods for the rest of the week.

Balanced Eating Made Simple!

- Eat as many whole foods as possible. This means unprocessed foods! If it comes in a box or a bag, it is processed.
- Eat a rainbow on your plate! Fill your plate with colorful veggies and fruits. This is a great way to get nutrient-dense foods in your daily diet.
- Eat protein, fats and unrefined carbohydrates at every meal. This includes snacks! Include small amounts of grass-fed animal protein and more veggies on your plate!
- Sea veggies, fermented foods, nuts and seeds daily
- Drink lots of good clean water. Filter it if possible.
- Eat slowly and with attention. This helps with digestion and helps keep us from overeating.
- Eat locally grown and seasonal foods when possible
- Smile, laugh and enjoy your food.

Some nourishing foods to choose from:
(Choose organic when possible)

- Veggies: kale, broccoli, zucchini, red peppers, salad greens, tomatoes, carrots, beets and all amazing colorful veggies
- Fruits: blueberries, raspberries, apples, bananas, and any other colorful fruit
- Protein: Organic chicken and turkey, grass fed beef, wild salmon, organic protein powder, eggs, organic yogurt, legumes and kefir
- Fats: avocados, coconut oil, shredded coconut, olive oil, seeds, nuts and grass fed butter
- Grains- quinoa and rice- pre-soaked
- Fermented foods: sauerkraut, kefir, miso and kimchi
- Sea veggies: kombu, arami and nori

Eating a variety of the foods mentioned above will help insure that you and your kids are getting your daily needed vitamins and minerals.

Other info:

You can add a small piece of kombu to your grains and beans before cooking when adding your fresh water after rinsing. This can add more minerals and make the foods more alkaline. You can buy kombu (a nutrient dense sea vegetable) at Whole Foods Market.

You can also sprout your grains and legumes to add even more nutritional value to them. This is a simple process that I encourage you try. You can find out more about sprouting in the Nourishing Connection Cookbook by Cathryn Couch and JoEllen DeNicola - visit www.Ceresproject.org to purchase the cookbook.

Simple Meal Planning: "Sunday Fun Day Cooking"

Inspiring, quick and simple meal planning and food prep ideas that can help make your week less stressful AND make sure you are eating nutrient dense foods daily. Choose a day of the week like "Sunday" to meal plan, prep and cook for your week.

What to do on "Sunday Fun Day"?

1. Plan some simple and quick meals for your week. Make sure to make extra food so that you can have leftovers. Also, make extra food so you can freeze if possible.

2. Sit down for a few minutes and take inventory in your cabinets and fridge to see what you may need to get at the grocery store. Plan out what stores, farmers markets, etc. you need to go to in order to get all the ingredients for the meals you have planned. Shop early or on the day of cooking!

Food Prep:

1. Concentrate on healthy fats, proteins and lots of colorful veggies. Make each "snack" a mini-meal of healthy fats, proteins and veggies. Plan 2-3 easy breakfast ideas, 2-3 lunch ideas, 2-3 dinner ideas and a few things you can snack on daily.

2. Wash and cut up veggies and fruits. Place in glass container and refrigerate. Wash some lettuce or salad greens and place in fridge. By prepping your veggies, you will eat more during the day.

3. Grill, bake or boil some chicken breasts and place in glass container to store in fridge. This way you have

some animal protein to toss in salads, sandwiches or just to nibble on for quick energy.

4. Soak 10   2 cups of gluten free grains (soak 12 hours or overnight). Drain and rinse grains. Cook these grains in fresh water, chicken or veggie broth and place in container and refrigerate. Some gluten free grains are quinoa, millet, rice, and amaranth. These grains provide protein, vitamins and minerals and are low on the glycemic index.

5. Hard0 boil some eggs and store in a container in refrigerator. These are easy and "grab on the go" protein snacks. You can also make them into a quick egg salad and place them on crackers, bread or rye crisps.

6. Sauté some greens (kale, chard, collards or spinach). Put olive oil on after you sauté. Store in a container in the refrigerator. You can add these greens to eggs, grains, or anything you would like.

7. Roast some root veggies. Sweet potato, red potato and parsnips. Bake at 350 degrees for 1 hour with a light olive oil and salt.

8. Use a Crock Pot. These are so fabulous! Place ingredients, turn on low and enjoy when you get home from a long day. I love my Crock Pot!

Soaking Beans, Grains and Nuts Made Simple!

It is very important that you soak your beans and legumes before you eat them. Pre-soaking beans (AKA legumes) and grains are very important for your health and digestion. By soaking beans and grains, it neutralizes the phytic acid and makes the beans/grains/nuts more alkaline. This pre-soaking process may help with better digestion and better absorption of the nutrients. Here are the approximate times to soak and some simple tips I use:

Simple Soaking Tips:
Pre-soak with water, rinse well and toss out the old water, place beans or grains in pot. Add fresh water and cook.

Bean Soaking Times:
Soak all lentils, beans, and split peas overnight (10-12 hours). I sometimes soak them for 24 hours (except lentils they are fine at 10-12 hours).

Grain Soaking Times:
Soak quinoa, millet, and rice overnight (10-12 hours).

Nuts and Seeds basic info: Nuts and seeds also contain the enzyme inhibitor phytic acid. Soaking them and dehydrating them may help with digestion and absorption of nutrients. Make sure to soak and rinse well before consuming. Use a dehydrator to dry them for 1-3 days OR cook in oven at approximately 150 degrees on a baking sheet for 8 hours. *Yes, soaking Nuts and Seeds is hard to do, even I don't always get around to it – but as long as we try to soak even one batch a week we are making improvement!*

Nuts and Seeds Soaking Times:
Walnuts and Cashews- 4-6 hours
Almonds-12 hours
Seeds 2-4 hours

Inflammation Made Simple!

Inflammation can play a huge role in so many illnesses like cancer, diabetes, digestive issues and heart disease. It's very important that we try to help our bodies stay un-inflamed so we can try to prevent these issues.

Some simple ways to help with inflammation are:

- Minimize or stop stress.
- Eat an anti-inflammatory diet.
- Eat anti-inflammatory spices like turmeric, ginger and fresh garlic.
- Cut out refined sugar - choose low glycemic fruit instead (see page Sugar Made Simple)
- Eat unrefined grains vs. refined grains; refined grains turn to sugar so much faster!
- Consume Omega-3's daily- Flax oil, cod liver oil and/or chia seeds.
- Cut out process foods. Don't eat out of a box!
- Eat the color of the rainbow with veggies and fruits on your plate.
- Enjoy life more, laugh, be grateful and smile lots during the day!

Some alkaline foods:
Almonds
Leafy greens
Avocados
Seaweed
Lentils
Grass-fed meats and raw dairy

Some acidic foods:
Alcohol/soda
Coffee/black tea
White sugar/processed foods
Meats and dairy that are NOT grass-fed

Sugars Made Simple!

Not all sugar is the same. So pay attention to those food labels! Some sugar is better for our bodies than others.

- Avoid artificial sweeteners like sucralose, aspartame & saccharin. These are chemicals and can produce inflammation in the body and potential health risks.
- Agave is a highly processed sugar. It's considered a source of concentrated fructose. Processed sugars=inflammation!
- Processed or refined sugars have little to no nutrient value. To much sugar can lead to an overload on the liver and blood sugar spikes.
- Eliminate all processed sugar from your diet. This includes white sugar, corn syrup, and high fructose corn syrup.
- Use minimally processed sugars as they contain some nutrients. These include: coconut palm sugar, date sugar, maple syrup, local honey (best if its raw/unheated as heating destroys the healthy enzymes) and molasses. Don't use honey for kids under one year of age!
- Sweeten with whole, natural, fresh or frozen fruits. Fruits have a lot of vitamins and minerals. Bananas & mangos are considered higher sugar fruits. Berries are the best choice since they are lower in sugar/fructose.
- Try stevia, an herb. It's very sweet but has little/no effect on blood glucose/sugar levels. Use just a drop or two or a pinch as it's very sweet!
- Try to keep sugar intake down to 15-20 grams or less per day for kids (and adults). This is just a good point of reference in my opinion!

Some nourishing options to help with sugar cravings:

- Eat some protein and fats - nuts, seeds and avocados
- Drink a little decaf chai tea with almond milk
- Eat some fresh berries - lower glycemic
- Eat 1-2 squares of dark chocolate 70% or higher
- Eat a spoonful of coconut butter and or nut butter

Carbohydrates Made Simple!

All Carbohydrates break down into sugar.

There are GOOD carbs – unrefined
There are BAD carbs – refined

Unrefined carbs are the best
- They are slow digesting and don't seem to cause a huge blood sugar spike.
- They have lots of good vitamins, minerals and fiber.

Some Unrefined Carbs are:
- Whole Grains
- Root Veggies - Turnips and Parsnips
- Broccoli
- Spinach
- Eggplant
- Sweet Potatoes
- Carrots
- Fruits

Beans are legumes but also are unrefined carbs – it is very important to soak beans overnight to remove the phytic acid coat to help with better digestion.
- Lentils
- Black beans
- Kidney beans
- Adzuki beans

Some Simple/Refined carbs are:
- Cookies/Cakes/Pastries
- Sugar
- Corn syrup
- Packaged cereals
- White flour

Protein Made Simple!

Protein is important to eat throughout the day to support energy levels and to maintain proper blood sugar levels. A serving size of protein is approximately the size of the palm of your hand. Eat a little protein with your meals and snacks to feel your best!

Some Plant Foods Protein Options:
- Almonds
- Chickpeas
- Tempeh
- Walnuts
- Kale
- Quinoa
- Lentils
- Hemp seeds
- Black beans
- Protein powder - hemp, rice or pea protein

Some Animal Foods Protein Options:
- Grass-fed beef
- Grass-fed gelatin
- Organic eggs
- Organic yogurt
- Organic chicken
- Bacon
- Organic cheese
- Kefir
- Protein powder - grass-fed whey

Important Tip:
If you are a vegetarian you may want to consider taking a B12 supplement. Most plant foods don't naturally contain the vitamin B12. You can also consume nutritional yeast. (*Crazy Sexy Diet by Kris Carr* Pg. 69)

Kale is a Superfood!

Fermented Foods Made Simple!

Eating a variety of fermented foods can help with building a stronger digestive tract. Add these simple foods that contain healthy microflora and probiotics to your daily diet.

Kefir - Fermented dairy product rich in antioxidants and probiotics.

Yogurt - Contains natural probiotics.

Kimchi - Spicy pickled Korean vegetables.

Sauerkraut - Fermented cabbage provides lactobacilli bacteria.

Miso - Fermented paste that contains live cultures.
Try garbanzo miso if avoiding soy

Tempeh - Cultured soybean product that's high in protein.

Remember that over 70% of your immunity lives in your gut. Adding fermented foods to your diet can help with immunity for adults and KIDS.

Fats Made Simple!

Fats are super important for your overall health! Most of our brain is composed of fats.

- Avoid saturated fats that are in processed foods.
- Enjoy monounsaturated fats like olive oil, avocados and nuts.
- Enjoy high quality saturated fats like raw cheese, grass-fed butter and ghee in moderation.
- Polyunsaturated fats (Omega-3 and 6's) like wild salmon, chia seeds, flax seeds, flax oil, and olive oil.
- Try to avoid polyunsaturated fats like canola oil and vegetable oil.
- Fats are important for proper brain function.
- Nuts and seeds are packed with protein and energy.
- Essential fatty acids are very important for a well functioning nervous system and overall immunity. These include Omega-3's and Omega-6's. Many people are low on Omega-3's.

Some fats to enjoy daily:
- Avocados and/or avocado oil
- Olive oil
- Coconut oil
- Nuts
- Seeds
- Nut butters
- Organic eggs
- Grass-fed butter/ghee
- Organic yogurt
- Kefir

Superfoods Made Simple!

Superfoods are foods that are nutrient-dense and provide a power-packed amount of nutrition in each and every bite. Enjoy these foods on their own or use them as add-ins to your favorites foods and recipes.

Some of my favorite Superfoods are:

Leafy Greens are loaded with fiber and vitamins.

Blueberries are a low glycemic fruit and high in antioxidants.

Chia SEEDS are rich in plant based Omega-3's, protein, fiber and minerals.

Almonds contain protein, fats, fiber and good for you heart!

Grass-fed Gelatin - Contains protein, helps aid toxin removal and helps with joint pain. *(See Berry Gummy Treats on page 189.)*

Dairy free dark chocolate is loaded with antioxidants. Please get 70% or higher dark chocolate to enjoy these benefits.

Avocados are rich in good fats, folate and glutathione.

Wild Salmon is rich in Omega-3's.

Sweet Potatoes are loaded with vitamins A, C and potassium.

Kefir is a wonderful fermented food rich in probiotics - great for the gut!

Enjoy these wonderful Superfoods daily!

Reading Packaged Food Labels Made Simple

It's best to limit how much processed or packaged foods we eat. Instead, eat whole foods that are nourishing and nutrient dense and come from the earth. However, it is nearly impossible to never eat processed foods these days (especially for us BUSY people). Here are some simple suggestions for making reading food labels easier.

What TO Look FOR:
- Try to find packaged foods with minimal ingredient lists.
- It's nice to be able to recognize the ingredients and not have to ask yourself "what is that"?
- If you can find packaged foods with Avocado oil and/or coconut oil that would be a healthier choice, as they do not go rancid/bad as fast as other oils.
- Just because a package says "gluten free" does not mean it's healthy for you. Check the labels on everything! Sometimes the gluten free goodies are loaded with lots of sugar and a long ingredient list.

What TO STAY AWAY FROM
- Stay away from high fructose corn syrup, corn syrup, hydrogenated oils, artificial coloring/dyes and MSG. These are not nourishing at all and have been linked to increased risk for disease and inflammation in the body.
- Be careful with "Industrial Seed Oils" in packages foods. Some of these are canola oil, safflower oil, corn, peanut, sunflower and soy. **These oils may also say "vegetable" oil so you think they are healthy but they are not.** They are not nutrient dense oils. These Omega-6 oils are less stable and can oxidate very quickly (AKA go rancid quickly and oxidation can cause inflammation in the body). These oils are very hard to avoid in almost all packaged foods!
- Always check labels for SUGAR. Almost all processed foods contain some sugar. Most BREAD also contains some type of sugar!

Self-Care Made Simple

Yes, you are reading this right: self-care! Something we all should be doing more of but NEVER have the time because we are all too BUSY. So here are a couple of Simple ways to nourish your mind and body with little time.

Self-care can be hard to fit into our daily life, but it's probably us busy parents who need it the most! Also, I believe when we as parents actively are doing self-care we can be more patient and present with our children. Sounds great right? Then why don't we do self-care daily? I struggle with this one BIG time. I believe it's because sometimes self-care adds to our "to do" list and we all know how that one goes! So here are some SIMPLE suggestions to get a little self-care for busy people!

All of these suggestions can be done in 5-10 minutes to start then work your way up in time when you're ready:

- Take a 10-minute warm bath with Epsom salt. Epsom salt can help relax the body!
- Do some sort of meditation for 5 minutes in the morning when you are waking up. This can be saying a simple mantra like "you are calm and relaxed" said over and over again. This can help be in the present moment
- Do some slow and deep breathing! This resets the nervous system and activates your parasympathetic nervous system.
- Have a quick lunch with a good friend, hug someone and laugh. This all raises oxytocin, "the love hormone".
- Take a 5-10 minute walk and be in nature.
- Drink a cup of warm herbal tea and listen to some soothing music.
- Write in a gratitude journal at night before bed for 5 minutes. Choose 3-5 things you are grateful for during that day or week.

- Eat some comfort food that is nourishing to your soul. For me I love toast with almond butter and a smidge of strawberry jam - so good!

A couple self-care ideas that take a little more time and planning but are amazing (find local or national practitioners in the resource guide at the end of my cookbook):

- Have some acupuncture done! Amazing and helps with everything in my opinion
- Get adjusted by a chiropractor or cranial therapist. Helps reset the nervous system and lots of other nourishing benefits
- Take a self care day - day spa, shopping, solo lunch, soak in bath, long relaxing drive, day at the beach... anything that feeds your soul
- Meet with an herbalist or functional medical practitioner to make a game plan for overall health and wellness plan individual to you
- Inner Balance App - Heartmath.com - helps reduce stress!

Kids Setting the Dinner Table: Why is it so Important?

About a year ago when Nylah turned three we had her start setting the table. This is a big deal for her and she takes it VERY seriously. She asks now to set the table and loves to have a special little job. Every night we eat at about 6 p.m. together as a family at the table. This is an important time for us to connect and enjoy time together after a busy day.

We cook nourishing foods and it is important to us to also make them look nice on the plates before we enjoy our food. We also love our table (or sometimes a floor picnic blanket table) to look simple but nice. By having Nylah set the table, we can talk about how nice it looks and how proud we are of her helping contribute. Here are some simple tips for kids helping to set the table:

- Have a place that they can go and get all the necessary table settings needed.
- Nylah goes to our special cabinet that holds all the napkins and placemats.
- Leave the plates in the kitchen and have adults dish up and place full plates on set table - less glass to clean up if an accident happens!
- Let them place the drink cups at the table.
- Let them place placemats and napkins wherever they want (within reason) on the table - this is THEIR table to set!

Kids want to be involved and what a perfect way to get your kids excited about their food by having them set the dinner table.

Nylah "Big Girl" Setting The Table

My Kids Won't Eat Greens - *HELP ME Please!*

I get this question asked a lot especially by the families at the preschool where I teach nutrition. The question is "my kids won't eat any greens and are so picky what can I do" Here are my simple suggestions for getting more nourishing foods in your kids diets:

- Make food fun and relax about it...
- Use cookie cutters to make fun shapes for sandwiches.
- Use dried fruit, olives or blueberries to decorate fun food faces.
- If your child does not like a food, don't make a big deal about it and reintroduce it again a few days or weeks later.
- Make lots of food and introduce your child to many different foods and have them make their choice of what they want to try - this way you have lots of left overs for the rest of the week and everyone in the family is HAPPY.
- Amazing Grass Superfoods powder comes in berry and chocolate for kids and it does not turn your smoothie green!
- Make some fun and nourishing "green" juice. Make a veggie juice with cucumber, celery and ½ apple - all organic!
- Make some kale pesto and have them dip veggies into it. They love to dip!
- Make food fun by decorating it. This may help get your kids interested in eating more greens and colorful veggies.

Here are some ideas for decorating food and making it FUN for kids.

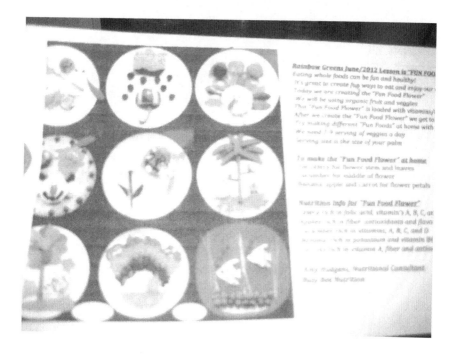

Cooking With Your Kids Rocks!

Why is cooking with your kids so important? Here are my simple thoughts:

- Cooking together can create an amazing connection.
- Learning early math skills - counting and measuring.
- This can be a time to talk about where food comes from.
- Builds confidence - little children love to be "helpers".
- Encourages an openness to try new foods.
- Builds teamwork.
- Helps with patience.

My little sweet story:

When my daughter Nylah was very young we would have her help with unloading the veggies from the grocery or farmers market bags into the fridge. We made a special space for her to unload the colorful veggies and fruit.

As she unloaded, we talked about what color the veggies were, where they grow and why they are good for us. We would smell, feel and touch the veggies together as they went into the fridge. Nylah is four now and we still do this from time to time. It's a great way to teach your kids about healthy food. Nylah felt so important that she had her own "special job" of unloading the colorful veggies into the fridge.

I encourage all of you to try cooking with your kids. Cooking together can create such great memories and is SUPER FUN!

Diabetes Awareness - Childhood Obesity
By JoEllen DeNicola N.E

The American Medical Association (AMA), officially recognized obesity as a disease that requires strategies for prevention and medical treatment if necessary. (1) This is a major step towards understanding that what we eat does affect our health. What we eat in fact is the foundation for our health.

According to a report from the Reuters the American Medical Association has found obesity in the adult US population has doubled in the past twenty years. This finding notes that obese adults are at a higher risk for cancer, heart disease, type 2 diabetes as well as and other debilitating diseases. (2)

The AMA also stated that in *one generation the obesity rates for children have tripled!* In fact the statistics are startling. The Food Research and Action Center reports "About a quarter of 2-5 year olds and one-third of school-age children (including adolescents) are overweight or obese in the U.S." (3) Our Nation's obese youth are at risk for type 2 diabetes, heart disease, endocrine and cholesterol issues, as well as cancer. Something that was almost not heard about just one generation ago is now true, our children are burdened with health issues that will challenge them throughout their lives.

With children becoming overweight so early in life their risk of Type 2 Diabetes increases. According to the Mayo Clinic report on risk factors for Type 2 Diabetes: **"being overweight is the primary risk factor in children."** Please note that though a child that is overweight is at risk, so are normal weight children that develop fatty organs from improper nutrition or that have other factors that put them at risk.

These other risk factors include:

- **Physical Activity Level:** Children who are inactive or have little activity are at higher risk for developing Type 2 Diabetes. The more active the child the more energy they burn, which means they are burning glucose sugars.
- **Family History:** Are there family members with Type 2 Diabetes? If so that increases a child's risk factors. This is especially of significance if it is a parent or a sibling.
- **A Child's Sex:** Girls are more at risk than boys.
- **Race:** African Americans, Hispanics, Native Americans, Asian Americans, and Pacific Islanders are at higher risk for Type 2 Diabetes than other races.

What can we do to help our children stay healthy? First off become an example of health to your children through your actions. You can create a culture of health in your family and spread that to your friends and community.

Children learn by example. Your job is to set the healthy example without being too anxious or overbearing. The entire family can participate in creating healthy meals and choose activities that support health. This may be a daily walk, bicycling to the store or a friends, park days, shopping at farmers markets, choosing whole food meals over fast foods, cooking together, taking time to relax and enjoy life together, being active in sports, and giving up processed foods and sugar for whole foods that include fruits, vegetables, sea vegetables, nuts and seeds, fermented and sprouted foods, whole grains, legumes, fresh fish and poultry, organic dairy, and grass fed white meats.

Healthier choices are proactive choices. You are deterring poor health and promoting an active body and mind.
The recipes in this cookbook provide you with simple ways to create nutrient rich dishes. Changing the consumer habits, food choices, and activity and relaxation patterns of your family is in your hands. Choose well.

References

1. *American Medical Association Recognizes Obesity as a Disease.* Rudd Radar. July 19, 2013. http://www.yaleruddcenter.org/american-medical-association-recognizes-obesity-as-a-disease

2. Carey, Nick., *U.S. doctor group votes to recognize obesity as a disease. Reuters. June 18, 2013.* http://www.reuters.com/article/2013/06/18/usa-doctors-obesity-idUSL2N0EU2AB20130618

3. Ogden, C. L., Carroll, M. D., Kit, B.K., & Flegal, K. M. (2012). Prevalence of obesity and trends in body mass index among U.S. children and adolescents, 1999-2010. Journal of the American Medical Association, 307(5), 483-490. Retrieved from http://frac.org/initiatives/hunger-and-obesity/obesity-in-the-us/

4. Type 2 Diabetes in Children. Mayo Clinic http://www.mayoclinic.com/health/type-2-diabetes-in-children/DS00946/DSECTION=risk-factors

Debra Merritt Bruflat

Chapter 2: Beautiful Breakfast

After fasting all night when you were sleeping, it is very important to "break the fast" with a nourishing breakfast...Enjoy!

Avocado Boats

This simple recipe is packed with healthy fats and protein and can be enjoyed for breakfast or a snack.

Ingredients
2 ripe avocados
1 medium tomato, chopped
2 tsp goat cheese
2 tsp pumpkin seeds, chopped
¼ cup chopped cilantro
Olive oil
Himalayan salt
Pepper

Directions
1. Cut open and pit avocados.

2. Mix tomato, goat cheese, pumpkin seeds and cilantro in small bowl.

3. Fill each avocado half with some of the tomato mixture.

4. Sprinkle olive oil, salt and pepper on top of each avocado half and serve.

Serves 4

Pumpkin Breakfast Cookies

Ingredients
1½ cups organic rolled oats
1½ bananas, chopped
1 cup mashed pumpkin (canned or fresh)
½ cup sliced almonds
2 tbsp shredded coconut
3-4 tbsp maple syrup
2 tbsp ground flax seeds
¼ cup chopped walnuts
1 tsp cinnamon, nutmeg and cardamom
¼ tsp sea salt
¼ cup dried cranberries (optional for added sweetness)

Directions
1. Preheat oven to 350°F.

2. Spray baking sheet with natural olive oil spray.

3. Combine pumpkin, banana, maple syrup, spices and salt in a mixing bowl and mix by hand until mostly smooth.

4. Add in oats, walnuts, almonds, flax seeds and shredded coconut and mix thoroughly. If mixture needs more moisture, add in ½ mashed banana or a couple tablespoons applesauce.

5. Form 10-12 small cookies and bake for 10-12 minutes.

Makes 10-12 cookies

Nutrition Tip: Oats are great for calming the nervous system. Buy gluten-free oats if avoiding gluten, since oats can be contaminated with gluten in the processing.

Breakfast Greens and Beans

Eat a rainbow of colors on your plate and feel plant strong!

Ingredients
Coconut oil
1 cup chopped kale
1 cup chopped spinach
1 cup chopped chard
1 clove chopped garlic
1 can BPA-free white beans
Sea salt
Pepper
Chili flakes
Cumin
Turmeric

Directions
1. Heat coconut oil in a frying pan over medium-high heat.

2. Sauté kale, spinach, chard and garlic together until softened.

3. Add beans, salt, pepper, chili flakes, cumin and turmeric and mix together. Serve and Enjoy!

Serves 2M 4

Nutrition Tip: Remember we need 7-9 servings of veggies per day. This recipe is a great way to get them into your breakfast.

Amazing Blueberry Granola

This recipe was inspired by *Nourishing Connections Cookbook.*

Ingredients

4 cups regular rolled oats
½ cup flax seeds
½ cup hemp seeds
1 cup chopped almonds
½ cup chopped walnuts
½ cup pumpkin seeds
3 tbsp melted coconut oil
2 tbsp honey
2 tbsp maple syrup
1 tbsp vanilla extract
2 tbsp cinnamon
1 tbsp ground cardamom
Pinch of salt
1 cup unsweetened shredded coconut
¼ cup goji berries
½ cup of dried blueberries

Directions

1. Preheat oven to 300°F.
2. In a bowl, stir the oats, seeds and almonds together.
3. In a saucepan, heat coconut oil over low heat. Whisk in honey, maple syrup, spice and salt.
4. Place granola on a large greased cookie sheet and spread mixture out so it evenly coats cookie sheet. Bake for 15 minutes. Stir well and bake for another 15 minutes. The granola can be baked longer if you desire. Watch it closely so it does not burn. You want granola to be golden brown and dry.
5. Cool, then stir in goji berries, coconut and blueberries. Granola can keep for months in an airtight container.
6. Serve with milk or yogurt, or just eat a little handful plain.

Cranberry Walnut Scones

This recipe is by JoEllen DeNicola

Ingredients

¼ cup maple syrup
¾ cup butter
2 ¾ cup spelt flour (or a gluten-free flour mixture)
Pinch of sea salt
2 tsp baking powder
¾ cup coconut milk or whole milk
1 cup toasted walnuts
½ cup cranberries

Directions

1. Preheat oven to 375°F.

2. Mix butter and dry in ingredients in food processor, blending well. Add toasted walnuts and pulse.

3. Pour into a bowl, make a well and slowly add the coconut milk.

4. Roll out into a round and cut into 10-12 wedges. The less handling, the better.

5. Place onto a parchment paper covered cookie sheet.

6. Bake for about 20 minutes.

Makes 6 larges scones

Nutrition Tip: Walnuts are a source of Omega-3 and Omega-6 fatty acids.

Grass-Fed Steak and Eggs

This quick breakfast is packed with amazing protein.

Ingredients
2 organic eggs
½ cup of grass-fed steak, precooked
1 cup of organic mixed greens, washed
Salt
Pepper

Directions
1. Fry eggs in coconut oil in a pan over medium heat.

2. Place cooked eggs on a plate with a few pieces of pre-cooked steak.

3. Add a handful of mixed greens, salt and pepper on top and enjoy!

Serves 2-3

Nutrition Tips: Grass-fed beef is packed with nourishing Omega-3's.

Pre-cook steak or use "last nights" leftovers to make this a 10-minute breakfast!

Appleberry Muffins
This recipe is by JoEllen DeNicola

Ingredients
1½ cups whole wheat flour, finely milled
Other options: spelt, brown rice, oat, barley, tapioca or quinoa flour
Pinch of cloves, ground
¾ tsp cinnamon
1½ tsp baking powder - non-aluminum
½ tsp baking soda
½ tsp salt
¼ cup coconut oil or walnut oil
½ cup molasses
1 cup applesauce
½ cup goji berries or cranberries
¼ cup chopped walnuts

Directions
1. Preheat the oven to 350°F.

2. Grease and flour one 12-cup muffin tin.

3. Sift the dry ingredients and add the oil, molasses and applesauce. Mix well.

4. Add the goji berries and chopped walnuts.

5. Fill the muffin cups half way.

6. Bake for 20 minutes.

Makes 12 muffins

Banana Currant Breakfast Cookies

Ingredients
2 bananas
½ cup almond butter
1 egg
½ tsp vanilla
½ tsp cardamom
¼ tsp sea salt
1 tbsp cinnamon
¼ cup shredded coconut
¼ cup currants

Directions
1. Preheat oven to 350°F.

2. Combine all ingredients until well blended.

3. Using a tablespoon, drop cookies onto a greased baking sheet.

4. Bake for 10-12 minutes until golden brown on the bottom.

Serves about 20 cookies

Nutrition Tip: Almond butter is full of protein and healthy fats.

Almond Flour Pancakes

Ingredients
2 organic eggs
¼ cup honey
1½ cups almond flour
¼ tsp sea salt
½ tsp cinnamon
¼ tsp cardamom
½ tsp baking soda
Coconut oil or grass-fed butter

Directions
1. Mix eggs and honey together in a high-speed blender.

2. Add almond flour, salt and baking soda to egg mixture and blend.

3. Place a small amount of coconut oil or butter in pan over medium heat.

4. Spoon pancake batter into hot pan.

5. Flip when pancakes form little bubbles.

Serves 8-10

Important Reminder: Do not feed honey to children under one year old! The live bacteria can cause botulism in infants.

Nourishing Smoothie Bowls

The idea for this "smoothie bowl" is to eat it with a spoon in a bowl (not drink it in a glass) and add some amazing toppings to enjoy!!

Ingredients
8 oz. coconut or almond milk - add more liquid if you want it thinner
¼ cup chia seeds or less if desired
½ cup frozen fruit
¼ banana
½ avocado

Directions
1. Add coconut milk (or liquid) first then all the other ingredients into a blender and blend until smooth!
2. Pour into a bowl.
3. Top with above goodies and enjoy!!

Toppings
These go on after smoothie is poured in the bowl. Use as many as you want to add bright colors and added nutrition to your bowl.

Handful of each:
Chopped almonds
Shredded coconut
Sliced Kiwis
Goji berries

Sliced bananas
Chopped apples
Blueberries
Pumpkin seeds
Granola

Fun Fact: Chia seeds are loaded with healthy Omega-3's, protein and fiber...and they make things thicker! Perfect for this smoothie bowl! These smoothie bowls are great when you want to add QUICK nourishment into your busy day.

Simple Turkey Breakfast Hash

Ingredients
1 pound ground turkey
1 cup chopped zucchini
½ cup shredded sweet potatoes
½ cup chopped kale
1-2 tbsp of olive oil (butter, ghee or coconut oil)
salt and pepper to taste
½ tsp cumin
½ tsp turmeric

Directions
1. Place olive oil in pan cook on medium to high heat

2. Add zucchini, sweet potatoes, kale salt, pepper, cumin and turmeric and sauté until soft

3. Cook ground turkey in separate pan on stovetop until fully cooked

4. Combine veggies into turkey pan and cook together for a few minutes

Cooking Tip: You can add any crunchy veggie like broccoli, cauliflower, green beans, and carrots. This recipe can be made ahead of time and warmed up in the morning. Super easy and can make breakfast (or snacks) simple for the whole busy week!

Serves 4-6

Breakfast Bowl Made Simple

Ingredients
1 cup cooked quinoa (or rice) - precooked
1 can black beans
1 chopped tomato
¼ cup chopped cilantro
Handful of chopped onion
½ chopped avocado
Optional: Salsa and/or fried or scrambled egg on top!

Directions
Place all of the above ingredients in a big bowl and enjoy!
Heat quinoa and beans beforehand.

Cooking Tip: The purpose of this simple breakfast bowl is to be able to have everything **cooked up a head of time** and just be able to chop a couple fresh items and throw together quick for those busy mornings... This is also a great snack, lunch or dinner recipe!

Serves 2-4

Simple Baked Oatmeal

Ingredients
2 cups organic rolled oats
1½ tbsp cinnamon
½ tsp cardamom
½ tsp sea salt
1 tbsp chia seeds
¼ cup goji berries
2 tbsp ground flax meal
½ cup raspberries
2 cups almond milk or coconut milk
1 tsp vanilla extract
2-3 tbsp pure maple syrup

Directions
1. Preheat oven to 350°F.

2. Combine oats, salt, cinnamon, cardamom, goji berries, flax, and chia seeds in a large bowl. Add berries, non-dairy milk, vanilla, and maple syrup. Mix well.

3. Spread mixture into an 8-inch square baking dish. Bake for approximately 25 minutes.

4. After it cools, cut into little squares and enjoy!

Makes 15-20 squares

Cooking Tip: Serve with organic yogurt on top and a dash of cinnamon for an extra treat. Make day before and warm up in the morning!

Green Eggs

Ingredients
Coconut oil
4 organic eggs
1 clove garlic
½ bunch arugula
1 cup chopped kale
Dash of chili flakes
Himalayan salt
Pepper

Directions
1. Scramble eggs with garlic and coconut oil over high heat.

2. When eggs are nearly cooked, add greens.

3. Top with pinch of salt, pepper and chili flakes.

Serves 4

Leftovers for Breakfast

Eat last night's leftover dinner for a hearty breakfast. Leftovers for Breakfast are simple, more nourishing, especially if you can work in those vegetables and a BIG time saver for a busy family on rushed mornings...

Some examples of Leftovers for Breakfast are:

- Cooked chicken and warm greens

- Breakfast salad: leftover salad with warmed sweet potatoes on top

- Grass-fed beef stew

- Turkey burger patty with ½ avocado

- Left over frittata

- Quinoa with pumpkin seeds and goat cheese

Nutrition Tip: Considering you have fasted ALL night, it is great to have a balanced breakfast full of protein, healthy fats and unrefined carbohydrates. It is okay to eat dinner for breakfast!

Simple Muesli

Ingredients
2 cups rolled oats
2 cups almond milk
¼ cup pumpkin seeds
¼ cup chopped walnuts
1 chopped banana
¼ cup goji berries
Cinnamon
Cardamom

Directions
1. Put dry oats in a medium bowl and add almond milk.

2. Stir and combine and place in fridge overnight.

3. The next morning, add the rest of the ingredients.

4. Mix well and enjoy!

Serves 6

Nutrition Tip: Walnuts are a great source of Omega-3s.

Simple Sweet Nourishing Toast

This sweet toast can be eaten for breakfast, snack or after dinner treat.

Ingredients
2 pieces of gluten-free toast
Almond butter
Coconut oil
Cinnamon
Cardamom

Directions
1. Toast two pieces of gluten-free toast.

2. Spread almond butter and coconut oil on toast while it is still hot.

3. Sprinkle cinnamon and cardamom on top and enjoy!

Serves 2

Nylah's Nourishing Applesauce

Ingredients
½-1 cup organic applesauce
Handful of goji berries
1 tablespoon coconut butter
¼ teaspoon cinnamon

Directions
1. Place applesauce in small bowl

2. Add all above ingredients on top and enjoy!

This breakfast treat is super easy and adds some amazing good fats from coconut butter, fiber from the applesauce and goji berries are a superfood!! Enjoy this nourishing treat as a breakfast side or even a dessert!

Simple Veggie Scramble

Ingredients
4-6 organic eggs
½ cup chopped kale
¼ cup chopped cilantro
½ yellow onion, diced
1 clove chopped garlic
2 medium zucchini, diced
¼ tsp sea salt
¼ tsp pepper
½ tsp chili flakes (optional)
1 tbsp butter, ghee or coconut oil

Directions
1. Sauté all veggies in butter, ghee or coconut oil on medium-high heat.

2. Add salt, pepper and chili flakes and cook until slightly soft.

3. Place all veggies and spices in a bowl and set aside.

4. Scramble eggs with grass-fed butter or coconut oil.

5. Add veggies from the bowl to the eggs just before they are fully cooked.

Serves 4

Nutrition Tip: Garlic has great immune system booting qualities.

Bacon and Egg Muffins (Grain- and Gluten-Free)

This recipe is by Katja Heino with *Savory Lotus*
(www.savorylotus.com).

Ingredients
10 eggs
½ tsp unrefined salt
several grinds of fresh black pepper
½ tsp garlic powder
1 tsp ghee or coconut oil
2 cups spinach, chopped
6 strips of cooked bacon, chopped into small pieces
2 tbsp fresh herbs, finely chopped (basil, cilantro, or parsley)
ghee or coconut oil for oiling muffin liners

Directions
1. Preheat oven to 350°F. Line a muffin pan with silicone liners or unbleached muffin liners. (I like to lightly oil my silicone liners.)

2. In a skillet, melt fat of choice over medium heat. Saute spinach for about a minute until it begins to wilt. Turn off heat. Add chopped bacon pieces and fresh herbs. Mix to combine.

3. In a large bowl, whisk together 10 eggs, salt, pepper, and garlic powder. Set aside.

4. Spoon spinach/bacon mixture into your prepared muffin cups. Pour the whisked eggs evenly over the mixture.

5. Bake for 20 minutes, or until toothpick inserted into the center comes out clean.

Sarah's Seed Cereal

Ingredients
¼ cup sunflower seeds
¼ cup pumpkin seeds or pepitas
¼ cup chopped almonds
¼ cup chopped walnuts
½ cup nondairy milk of choice
Optional for sweetness: chopped dates and/ or coconut flakes

Directions
Layer seeds, nuts, and sweet toppings in a bowl, pour in the milk, and enjoy the healthiest "cereal" ever, packed with plant proteins, Omega-3's, and healthy fats.

Tip: You can play with the exact ingredients, substituting whatever nuts and seeds happen to be in your cupboard.

This is also a great quick snack any time of day.

Eat Slow,
Balance
Happy Thoughts...

Chapter 3: Loveable Lunch

Almond Butter Sandwich Shapes

Ingredients
2 slices of sprouted whole grain bread OR gluten free bread
¼ cup almond butter
1 tsp of no-sugar-added jam

Directions
1. Spread almond butter and jam on bread and form into a sandwich.

2. Cut bread into fun shapes - squares, triangle, letters or circles.

Serves 1

Cooking Tip: Make eating fun and educational for kids by using shapes like numbers and letters. You can buy letter cut-outs OR use cookie cut-outs for even more fun with your sandwiches!

Avocado Pumpkin Seed Dip

Kids love to DIP things! Pack a few of these simple dips in your child's lunch box and let the nourishing fun begin!

Ingredients
1 avocado
2 tsp pumpkin seeds
Salt and Pepper

Directions
1. Mash avocado with a fork.

2. Add pumpkin seeds to avocado mash.

3. Add a dash of salt and pepper. Mix together and ENJOY!

Serve fun dips with:
- rice crackers
- rice cakes
- baby organic carrots
- organic celery pieces
- organic cucumber pieces

Serves 2-4

Cooking Tips: Please see the "Simple Side Dishes" and "Snacks" section of this cookbook fore MORE simple ideas for packing school lunches.

Leftovers are quick and easy options for lunch box packing!

Avocado Chicken Wrap

Wraps are simple and can be filled with anything you enjoy!

Ingredients
⅓ cup chopped chicken
1 rice tortilla
1 avocado, sliced
Handful of mixed lettuce greens
Handful of chopped cabbage
Handful of chopped cilantro
Olive Oil
Salt and Pepper, to taste
Pepper
Dash of balsamic vinaigrette

Directions
1. Place all ingredients in the rice tortilla.

Serves 2

Nutrition Tip: Try adding hummus or quinoa to wraps when you need that extra protein and healthy fat, or pesto for an extra kick of green vitamins and good fats.

Easy Egg Salad

Ingredients
4 organic eggs, hard boiled
2 tsp organic mayonnaise
½ cup chopped organic celery
¼ cup chopped pitted olives
Sea salt and pepper, to taste

Directions
1. Peel and chop eggs.

2. Combine all ingredients together and mix well.

3. Serve on:
   - Gluten-free or sprouted bread
   - Rice crackers
   - Rice cakes
   - Big pieces of carrots and celery for dipping

Serves 4

Cooking Tip: This is another great lunch box option. Eggs are packed with 7-9 grams of protein per egg. Make the day before to save time!

Chicken Lettuce Wraps

Ingredients
1 cup cooked chopped organic chicken
½ cup chopped organic tomatoes
½ chopped organic celery
¼ cup shredded carrots
2 pre washed organic butter lettuce leaves

Dressing:
1 tsp lemon juice
1 tsp apple cider vinegar
1 tsp olive oil
Salt and Pepper, to taste

Directions
1. Wash lettuce and all veggies first.

2. Place each veggie and chicken pieces in separate compartment in lunch box container.

3. Place dressing in separate little container so you can easily open and pour over lettuce wraps.

Serves 2

Cooking Tips: When packing these for lunch make sure you use a little lunch box where you can put all the veggies, cooked chicken, lettuce, and dressing in separate sections. Kids love to build things. Practice these lettuce cups one night together at dinner so that they know how to make them at lunch.

Pre-cook chicken and make dressing ahead of time to save time.

Nourishing BLTA Sandwich

Ingredients
4 slices sprouted bread or gluten free bread
½ pound cooked nitrate-free bacon
1 ripe avocado, peeled and pitted
2 ripe organic tomatoes
2 cups mixed salad greens
Organic mayonnaise, for spreading
Dijon mustard, for spreading
Olive oil

Directions
1. Cook bacon in pan over medium heat.

2. Toast bread and spread mayonnaise and Dijon mustard on toasted bread.

3. Place bacon, avocado, tomato and a handful of mixed greens on bread.

4. Use the extra mixed greens for a little side salad and garnish with olive oil.

Serves 2-3

Cooking Tips: Enjoy this simple and nourishing sandwich for breakfast, lunch or dinner!

Use butter lettuce to replace bread if desired.

Nut Butter Dip

Ingredients
½ cup almond, cashew or sunflower seed butter
1 tsp vanilla
1 tsp shredded coconut
¼ tsp cinnamon

Directions
1. Combine all together for a thick, nourishing dip.

Serve fun dips with:
- rice crackers
- rice cakes
- baby organic carrots
- organic celery pieces
- organic cucumber pieces

Serves 2-4

Simple Rice "Lunch Box" Pasta

Ingredients
½ bag of rice pasta or quinoa pasta
¼ cup chopped tomatoes
¼ cup chopped and pitted Kalamata olives
¼ cup shredded carrots
½ cup cooked organic chicken
2 tsp feta or goat cheese (optional)
2 tbsp olive oil
Salt and Pepper, to taste

Directions
1. Cook rice pasta, following instructions on bag.

2. Drain pasta and place in medium bowl.

3. Place all chopped veggies, chicken and feta into a bowl with pasta.

4. Place olive oil, salt and pepper on top and stir.

Serves 4

Cooking Tip: This is a great dinner or lunch option. If this is for a kid's lunch, place in an airtight container in their lunch box to keep fresh. You can make the day before to save time.

Turkey Miso Sandwich

This sandwich is a nutrition powerhouse, packed with healthy fats, protein, fermented food and greens!

Ingredients
2 pieces of sprouted OR gluten-free bread
Sliced "nitrate free" turkey
1 tsp miso paste
¼ of an avocado
Handful of your favorite greens
Dollop of mustard, to taste
Slice of tomato

Directions
1. Layer all ingredients in between two slices of bread and enjoy!

Serves 1

Yogurt Cucumber Dip

Ingredients
½ cup organic whole-fat Greek yogurt
¼ cup chopped cucumbers
1 tsp lemon juice
Salt and Pepper, to taste

Directions
1. Combine all together and enjoy!

Serve this refreshing dip with:
- rice crackers
- rice cakes
- baby organic carrots
- organic celery pieces
- organic cucumber pieces

Serves 2-4

Cooking Tip: Greek yogurt is thicker and makes a great base for a dip. It packs more protein too!

Mason Jar Chicken Pasta Salad

Ingredients
1 cup cooked brown rice pasta
¼ cup chopped cooked chicken
½ cup shredded or chopped carrots
½ cup arugula
¼ cup chopped tomatoes
Handful of goat cheese or feta
2 tbsp olive oil
1 tsp apple cider or balsamic vinegar
salt, pepper

Directions
1. Place all ingredients in a Mason jar, with pasta on the bottom and then layer it up. Put lid on.

2. If you are going to prep this the night before leave olive oil and vinegar out until the day you take it with you or place it in a little side jar to combine later.

3. Open jar, pour all of the jar contents into a bowl and enjoy, or just eat right out of the jar!!

Serves 1

Tips: This is a great way to prep for lunches, picnics or snacks on the go!! You can prep a few of these in different variations over the weekend for easy "quick to-go" meals. Also, I just buy a whole cooked chicken on the weekend and that way I can whip these up fast and know there is added protein from the chicken!

Cute Cucumber Sandwiches

Ingredients
1 medium organic cucumber
2-3 slices roasted turkey – deli meat
Dash of Dijon mustard
Handful of organic arugula
Salt and pepper to taste
Optional: sliced tomato

Directions
4. Wash and peel cucumber.

5. Slice in half long ways.

6. Place turkey, Dijon, arugula, salt and pepper in between two halves of cucumber.

7. Cut in half and enjoy your cucumber sandwich!

Serves 1

Fun tips: It is so easy to make these cucumber sandwiches and is a great way to get more veggies into your day. Kids love to help makes these and pack them in school lunches! FUN!

Easy Mini Pizzas

Ingredients
4-6 pieces of gluten-free bread or bread of choice
½ cup of organic canned tomato sauce
1 cup organic cheese, shredded
½ cup cooked ham or salami – chopped roughly
½ cup black chopped canned olives

Directions
1.Preheat oven to 425°F.

2.Line toast on a baking pan and bake for 5 minutes.

3.Take toast out and spread sauce evenly on each slice of toast.

4.Add above toppings evenly to each slice of toast (or topping of your choice)

5.Bake for 4 minutes or until cheese is melted. Cool a bit and Serve!

Optional toppings: green onions, pinnacle, fresh tomato, chopped zucchini or other veggies. Add more sauce or more toppings if you wish!

Serves 4-6

Fun Tips: Make this fun for kids buy placing all pizza ingredients in a muffin pan and letting kids decorate their own pizzas. This would be super fun for a chill night with the family or when having some kids over for a play date!

Chapter 4: Simple Snacks

Snacks should be seen as "mini meals" and eaten every 2-4 hours to support energy levels throughout the day. They should consist of small amounts of protein, good fats and unrefined carbohydrates.

Nut Butter Chia Seed Balls

Ingredients
½ cup almond butter or cashew butter
3 tbsp coconut butter
2 tbsp maple syrup
¾ cup regular rolled oats (not quick-cook)
¾ cup brown rice puffs (optional, may use rolled oats instead)
¼ cup dried fruit (cranberries, sour cherries, blueberries)
2 tbsp chia seeds

Directions
1. In a saucepan over medium heat begin to heat cashew butter, coconut butter and rice syrup.

2. Stir until loosened and smooth.

3. Remove from heat. Stir in oats, rice puffs, chia seeds and dried fruit.

4. Stir all ingredients together.

5. Make into little balls and drop them into mini paper cupcake or candy liners.

6. Place on baking sheet and refrigerate until set, about 15 minutes. Enjoy!

7. To store, refrigerate in an airtight container for up to one week.

Makes about 24 balls

Nutrition Tip: Add protein powder for an extra protein boost. Add it after cooking but before you roll into little balls.

Avocado Mash

Ingredients
Two ripe avocados
1 tsp flax oil
1 tsp olive oil
¼ tsp garlic salt
¼ tsp sea salt
¼ cup tomatoes, chopped
¼ cup cilantro, chopped
¼ cup onions, chopped (optional)
Squeeze of fresh lemon juice

Directions
1. Place the two ripe avocados in a bowl and mash up with a fork.

2. Add the rest of the ingredients and stir to combine.

Serves 2-4

Cooking Tip: Serve this with crackers, veggies or eat alone. Yummy!

Baked Oatmeal Bites

Ingredients
3 mashed bananas
1 cup of almond milk
2 organic eggs
1 tbsp baking powder
3 cups organic rolled oats
1 tsp vanilla extract
½ cup currants
½ cup dried cranberries
½ cup organic shredded coconut
1 tsp cinnamon

Directions
1. Preheat oven to 375°F.

2. Mix all ingredients together. Spray muffin pan with nona stick spray, or use liners.

3. Bake 15-20 minutes for mini muffins or 20-30 minutes for regular muffin pan. Check muffins around 15 minutes. You will see the edges get brown and they will be firm to touch when they are ready.

Makes approximately 15-20

These baked oatmeal bites came out good but a little bland if sweetened with banana, dried fruit and vanilla extract. If you wish to have a sweeter flavor, add one the following:
- ¼ cup maple syrup
- Use vanilla non-dairy
- Add some cut up dark chocolate

Nutrition Tip: These treats have protein and fiber in every tasty bite. Enjoy!

Baked Pita Chips

Ingredients
1 package of whole wheat pita bread- or gluten free
Olive oil
Sea salt, cumin and cayenne pepper

Directions
1. Preheat oven to 400°F.

1. Cut pita bread into little triangles. You can also use gluten-free pita bread.

2. Place pita triangles on a parchment-lined cookie sheet

3. Lightly drizzle triangles with olive oil.

4. Place sea salt, cumin and a pinch of cayenne in a little bowl and stir to combine.

5. Sprinkle salt mixture over the pita chips.

6. Bake for 6-8 minutes or until nice and crispy.

Serves 4-6

Cranberry Flax Granola Bites

Ingredients
½ cup slivered almonds or walnuts
½ cup flax seeds
½ cup shredded organic coconut
½ cup pumpkin seeds
1 cup dried cranberries
1½ cups rolled oats (not quick-cook)
1½ cups brown rice crisp cereal
½ cup brown rice syrup - add more for more sweetness
2 tbsp maple syrup
1 tsp. vanilla extract
½ tsp salt
1 tsp ground cinnamon
¼ tsp ground cardamom

Directions
1. Preheat oven to 325°F.
2. Spread almonds, flax seeds, coconut and pumpkin seeds on a cookie sheet and cook them for 6-8 minutes or until they start to get brown. In the meantime, grease a 9x13 inch baking dish with butter or melted soft coconut oil.
3. Combine rice cereal, oats, cranberries, and toasted ingredients in a big bowl.
5. In a small saucepan, heat all the syrups, salt, cinnamon, cardamom, and vanilla extract over medium heat, stirring to avoid burning.
6. Once syrups come to a light boil, continue to cook for an additional 3-5 minutes until syrup becomes thick.
7. Pour syrup over oats and nuts mixture and mix everything together so that the syrup coats everything in the bowl.
8. While the mixture is still warm, pour the contents of the bowl into the prepared baking dish.
9. Using a spatula, pat everything down so it's compacted. You can place parchment paper over the top and press down firmly so that the bars don't break when they cool and are cut. Cut into little bite size pieces and enjoy!
Makes approximately 20 bites

Banana Almond Butter Boats

Ingredients
1 banana
Some almond butter
Himalayan sea salt

Directions
1. Cut banana down the center.

2. Spread almond butter on one side.

3. Sprinkle Himalayan sea salt.

4. Put back together.

Serves 2-4 small bites

Cooking Tips: You can also use cashew butter or sunflower seed butter.

This recipe is a nice balance of sweet and savory.

Nutrition Tips: This recipe is a good source of protein!

Grain-Free "Just Seeds" Crackers

Ingredients
1 cup sunflower seeds, preferably soaked and dehydrated
½ cup pumpkin seeds, preferably soaked and dehydrated
½ cup sesame seeds, raw
1 tbsp fresh rosemary, finely chopped (or 1 tsp dried) OR
2 tbsp fresh cilantro (finely chopped)
½ tsp Celtic sea salt
5 tbsp filtered water
2 tbsp coconut oil, melted

Directions
1. Preheat oven to 325°F.

2. Place sunflower seeds into food processor and process until well ground into flour.

2. Add pumpkin seeds and pulse until pumpkin seeds are coarsely broken up.

3. Add the rest of the ingredients and pulse until well combined and starting to stick together to form a dough.

4. Roll out dough between two pieces of parchment paper to ¼ inch (or less) thick and score the crackers into desired sizes with a pizza cutter.

5. Bake for 20 to 25 minutes.

6. Allow to cool completely, then gently break along cut lines.

Makes about 24 small crackers

"No-Nut" Yummy Bites

Ingredients
1 cup pitted dates
1 tbsp chia sees
1 tbsp flax meal
1 tbsp organic cold pressed coconut oil
1 tbsp applesauce
¼ of a ripe banana
1 tbsp plus 2 cups unsweetened organic shredded coconut, divided

Directions
1. Place dates, chia seeds, flax meal, coconut oil, applesauce, banana and 1 tablespoon coconut in food processor and process until sticky and smooth.

2. Roll into small balls.

3. Spread the remaining two cups of coconut on a plate and roll the balls to cover.

4. Refrigerate and enjoy!

Makes approximately 15-20 balls

Cooking Tip: *Add protein powder, green powder, gogi berries, nutritional yeast or any dried fruit of your choice.*

Nourishing Nori Wraps

Ingredients
1 organic Nori seaweed sheet
1-2 cups brown rice, quinoa, amaranth or hummus
Avocado, thinly sliced
Cucumber, thinly sliced
Carrot, thinly sliced
Cilantro, to taste
Miso paste, to taste
1 tsp olive oil
1 tsp chia, sesame, pumpkin or hemp seeds

Directions
1. Cook grains 1 cup grain of choice and two cups water or broth.
2. Pre-soak grains for at least 1 hour-best soaked for 12 hours.
3. Drain grains, rinse and add fresh water or broth.
4. Cook until grains are soft -15-20 minutes depending on type of grain.
5. Spread cooked grain on nori sheet and add above ingredients in any order you choose. *There is so much you can do with these wraps!*

Nutrition Tips: Nori Seaweed has the highest mineral content of all sea veggies, brown rice is a great source of fiber, minerals, calcium, B vitamins and iron. Avocado is a great source of "good for you fats", cucumber is very cooling to the digestive system and cilantro is detoxifying.

Miso is a fermented food full of live enzymes and so it helps aid digestion.

Nourishing Snack Bars

Ingredients
2 cups almonds
1½ cups pitted dates
2 scoops rice protein powder
4 tbsp almond butter
2 tsp goji berries
2 tsps dried cranberries
¼ tsp cinnamon
¼ tsp cardamom
¼ tsp sea salt

Directions
1. Blend almonds and sea salt in a food processor until blended.

2. Add dates and process until mixture stick together.

3. Add almond butter, spices, protein powder and continue to pulse for 1-2 minutes.

4. Blend in dried fruit.

5. Press the mixture into a small rectangular baking dish that has been lined with parchment paper.

6. Let sit in the refrigerator for 15-20 minutes and cut into small bars.

Makes about 15 bars

Red Ants on a Log

Kids love ants on a log, and so do most adults!

Ingredients
½ cup almond butter
Handful of dried cranberries
6-8 stalks of organic celery
Himalayan salt or sea salt

Directions
1. Wash celery.

2. Spread almond butter inside celery.

3. Place dried cranberries on top.

4. Sprinkle salt on top, to taste.

Serves 4-6 small pieces

Nutrition Tip: Make these ahead of time for a quick protein snack.

Simple Trail Mix

Ingredients
1 cup almonds
1 cup pumpkin seeds
1 cup shredded coconut – make sure it is in big flakes
½ cup dried blueberries-or cranberries
½ cup goji berries

Directions
1. Place all above ingredients in a bowl and mix up.

2. Store in a Mason jar and enjoy!

Serves 4-6

Nutrition Tip: This is a great quick way to enjoy some fats and proteins on the go, just grab a handful when you're hungry in between meals for a long-lasting boost.

White Bean Hummus

You can substitute garbanzo beans in this recipe for traditional hummus.

Ingredients
1 15-ounce can of white beans OR soak and make your own white beans
½ cup sesame tahini (add more if you want)
2 garlic cloves
2 tbsp fresh lemon juice
1 tsp ground cumin
Splash of olive oil for smoother consistency (optional)
Salt (optional)

Directions
1. Place beans, tahini, lemon juice, garlic, cumin, and olive oil in food processor. Blend until creamy.

2. Add a little water or more olive oil if hummus is still not as creamy as you would like.

3. Taste the hummus and adjust to taste. I like to add some salt as I am blending the hummus.

Serves 4-6

Homemade Nut Butters

Ingredients
1 cup almonds, cashews, or a blend of your favorites
¼ tsp sea salt

Directions
1. Put almonds in a food processor.

2. Pulse until mixture begins to get creamy, it may take up to 15-20 minutes, so patience is key here!

3. Add salt, then pulse until you reach desired consistency.

Makes approximately 1 cup

Cooking Tip: If you want a sweeter almond butter you can add a teaspoon of honey or rice malt syrup.

Important Reminder: Do not feed honey to children under one year old.

Easy Hard-Boiled Eggs
This recipe is by Mike Hudgens.

Ingredients
1 dozen organic eggs
Filtered water

Directions
1. Place all eggs in a medium-size pot.

2. Cover eggs with water.

3. Heat water on high heat until boiling.

4. When water boils, cover pot and turn off heat.

5. Let sit for 20 minutes.

6. Pour water out, rinse with cool water until eggs are cool.

7. Store in refrigerator for up to 3 days.

Makes 12 boiled eggs.

Nutrition Tip: These are a simple protein snack. Eggs contain approximately 7 grams of protein per egg! Make these ahead of time for easy, quick snacks during the busy week.

Bean-Free Hummus

Ingredients
2 zucchinis, peeled and diced
½ cup tahini
¼ cup lemon juice
¼ cup olive oil
2 tsp sea salt
½ tsp ground cumin

Directions
1. Combine all in a high-speed blender and blend until creamy.

2. Serve with carrots, cucumbers and celery and enjoy!

Serves 4-6

Lemon Coconut Energy Bites
This recipe is created by Marissa Mowinckel
inspire_fitness

Ingredients
1½ cups cashews
1¼ cups pitted dates
2 tbsp fresh lemon juice
1 tsp lemon zest
¼ cup shredded coconut

Directions
1. Process all the ingredients in a food processor until it forms a dough.

2. Roll into bite-sized balls and place in the fridge for 1-2 hours. Store in fridge.

Grateful Granola Energy Bars

Ingredients
¼ cup melted coconut oil
3 tbsp almond butter
¼ cup flax meal
2 tsp maple syrup
1¼ cup organic applesauce
3 cups rolled oats
¼ cup dried cranberries
½ cup goji berries
¼ cup pumpkin seeds or slivered almonds
¼ tsp sea salt
½ tsp cinnamon

Directions
1. Preheat oven to 325°F.
2. In a medium mixing bowl combine all dry ingredients then set aside.
3. In a small saucepan over low heat melt coconut oil, almond butter and maple syrup until melted.
4. Combine heated mixture with dry mixture and stir until well combined.
5. Transfer the mixture to a baking pan lined with parchment paper.
6. Press mixture with your hands to create even surface – *it kind of looks like a meatloaf but flatter.*
7. Bake until golden brown, about 40-45 minutes.
8. Cool completely and then cut into little bars.
9. Store in airtight container in fridge.

Stuffed Avocados

Ingredients
1 avocado, cut in half and pitted
Handful already cooked chicken, chopped
1 small tomato chopped
Handful cilantro chopped
Dash of Dijon, mayo or apple cider vinegar
Salt and pepper to taste

Directions
1. Chop up chicken, tomato and cilantro and place in bowl.

2. Add a little Dijon, mayo or apple cider vinegar into bowl and mix up.

3. Fill each half avocado with above ingredients.

4. Top with a little Himalayan or sea salt and pepper and enjoy!

Fun Tip: Simple and easy stuffed avocados take no time at all to prep! You can enjoy for a snack or a simple and quick lunch.

Chapter 5: Simple Side Dishes

Cauliflower Rice

Ingredients
1 head organic cauliflower
1-2 tbsp grass-fed butter
1 tbsp coconut oil
½ tsp cumin
¼ tsp red chili flakes
Himalayan or sea salt
Pepper

Directions
1. Wash cauliflower and place florets in food processor and pulse until consistency of rice. You can also chop very fine if you don't have a food processor.

2. Place coconut oil and butter in pan on medium heat.

3. Place Cauliflower in pan and add salt, pepper, cumin and red chili flakes.

4. Stir and cover pan for 5-10 minutes or until softened.

Serves 4

Cooking Tip: Cauliflower rice can be used as a substitute for regular rice or pasta.

Nutrition Tips: Cauliflower is anti-inflammatory, as well as a good source of B vitamins and fiber.

If avoiding grains, cauliflower is a great nutrition-packed carb alternative!

Rainbow Cole Slaw

This recipe is by Mike Hudgens.

Ingredients

Cole Slaw:
1 head washed napa cabbage
1 cup purple cabbage
2 medium yellow beets
1 medium red beet
2 large organic carrots
5 large red radishes

Dressing:
¼ cup apple cider vinegar
⅓ cup olive oil
Sea salt, pepper, granulated garlic powder to taste

Directions

1. Shred or julienne vegetables and place in large bowl.

2. Mix dressing and pour over cole slaw. Mix well and enjoy!

Serves 6-8

Cooking Tip: Make a big batch of dressing ahead of time to save time and use on any salad.

Cilantro Basil Pesto

Kids love this pesto!

Ingredients
½ cup cilantro
1 cup of basil
1 clove chopped garlic
3 tbsp olive oil
¼ tsp pepper
¼ tsp cumin
¼ tsp sea salt
½ tsp red chili flakes (optional)

Directions
1. Place cilantro, basil, salt, pepper, garlic and cumin in food processor.

2. Blend and add olive oil slowly until blended.

Serves 2-4

Cooking Tips: Use this nourishing pesto as sauce for pasta, spread on sandwiches or as a dip.

Add ½ cup of kale to sneak in a few more greens.

Roasted Fall Veggies

Ingredients
2 sweep potatoes, cubed
2 potatoes, cubed
2 parsnips, cubed
2 large carrots, cubed
3 beets, cubed
1 turnip, cubed
1 cup fresh pumpkin (optional)

Directions
1. Prea   heat oven to 375°F.

2. Place all cut up root vegetables on a roasting pan.

3. Drizzle veggies with some olive oil and Himalayan sea salt.

4. Making sure they are evenly coated.

5. Place in oven for approximately 45 minutes to 1 hour.
Serves 4-6

Cooking Tip: You can line your roasting pan with parchment paper (not wax paper) for easy clean up.

Nutrition Tip: Enjoy lots of roasted root veggies in fall and winter. Root vegetables are very nourishing and grounding.

Savory Lemon Brussels Sprouts
This recipe is by JoEllen DeNicola

Ingredients
2 pounds Brussels sprouts
¼ cup butter
½ tsp dried savory
2 tbsp lemon juice
⅓ cup toasted cashews

Directions
1. Wash the Brussels sprouts and cut an "X" in the bottom of each one to allow in moisture.

2. Cover the bottom of a 3-quart saucepan with water. Add the Brussels sprouts and bring the water to a boil, then lower to simmer. Steam for 10 minutes or so and drain the water from the Brussels sprouts, leaving them in the pan.

3. Melt the butter and mix with the lemon juice and savory. You can add pepper and salt if you like.

4. Add the sauce to the Brussels sprouts and stir gently, coating each Brussels sprout.

5. Toast the cashews over a low flame. Garnish the Brussels sprouts with the warm, toasted cashews.

Serves 4-6

Simple Creamy Polenta

Ingredients
4 cups water
Sea salt to taste
1 cup organic polenta
3 tbsp grass-fed butter

Directions
1. Heat water and salt on high heat until water boils.

2. Wisk in the polenta.

3. Lower the heat to simmer and add butter.

4. Cook polenta for about 25 minutes, stirring occasionally.

5. Stir in extra sea salt if desired.

Serves 4

Cooking Tip: Add chopped tomatoes and parmesan cheese on top when cooked.

Sweet Potato Fries

Ingredients
3-4 med-large sweet potatoes
Olive oil
Himalayan or Sea Salt

Directions
1. Preheat oven to 375°F.

2. Peel and slice sweet potatoes into thick strips.

3. Place strips on a baking sheet.

4. Drizzle with olive oil lightly.

5. Bake for about 1 hour.

6. Sprinkle salt on the fries and let cool.

Serves 4-6

Nutrition Tip: Sweet potatoes are full of vitamin A.

Simple Pickles

Ingredients
3 pounds fresh pickling cucumbers (unwaxed)
3 tbsp of sea salt
1 bunch of fresh dill
1 medium head of peeled garlic
3 peppercorns
1 tbsp brown mustard seeds
2 bay leaves
Handful of grape leaves, washed

Directions
1. Place half the herbs and spices on the bottom of two clean quart Mason jars or a crock. Place washed cucumbers vertically into the jars so that they are packed in. Put the rest of the herbs and spices into the jar.
2. Dissolve the sea salt into one half gallon of pure water. This is the pickling brine. Pour the brine over the cucumbers so they are completely covered. You may have extra brine.
3. Place the grape leaves on top of the cucumbers. Weigh down the mixture with a plate or cup, or anything that will submerge the cucumbers.
4. Cover with a cotton cloth and store for 7-21 days, tasting them to be sure they are to your taste.
5. Remember to check for molds or foam daily. Remove them with a wooden spoon.
7. Store pickles in a covered jar in the refrigerator to slow the rate of fermentation.

Nutrition Tip: Live lacto-fermented foods are valuable aids for healthy digestion. The beneficial microbes that are available help create a healthy gut ecology. They also help to support the immune system.

Simple Sauerkraut
This recipe is by JoEllen DeNicola

Ingredients
5 pounds white cabbage
3 tbsp sea salt

Directions
1. Remove the outer leaves of the cabbage. Set aside to use later.
2. Rinse and core the cabbage. Slice the remaining cabbage into ¼ inch slices. You can make them thinner or thicker if you like.
3. In a crock or heavy glass bowl, add the sliced cabbage and the Sea salt mixing the salt so that it is equally distributed throughout the sliced cabbage. Let it set to begin the release of the juices.
4. Pound the cabbage with your fist, or a meat pounder, until it releases cabbage juice. You will know you have pounded enough if you press the cabbage down firmly with your hands and the juice covers the cabbage.
5. Pack the mixture into a crock pot and cover with the outer cabbage leaves that were set aside. Place a plate and a Mason jar filled with water on top of the leaves. Cover with a cloth.
6. Set the covered crock in a warm shelf out of the sunlight for 4-9 days, depending on the flavor you want and the warmth of the room. Check the flavor by tasting the kraut under the leaves.
7. Decant into glass jars. Remove any foam or molds from the top of the sauerkraut before lifting the top leaves. If there is a bit of white or blue molds just remove it. Be sure that your sauerkraut has brine, which is the salted cabbage juice to cover your kraut. If there is not enough, mix one quart water with 1 tbsp of salt and add to the kraut.
Makes 2.5 quarts

Sweet Potato Mash

Ingredients
2-3 sweet potatoes
Olive oil
Himalayan Salt
Cumin
¼ cup pumpkin seeds
Coconut oil, or grass fed butter

Directions
1. Preheat oven to 400°F.

2. Peel and cut up sweet potatoes.

3. Place sweet potatoes on baking sheet.

4. Drizzle with olive oil.

5. Bake for 45 minutes to 1 hour until very soft.

6. Mash sweet potatoes with fork.

7. Add salt, cumin and coconut oil.

8. Sprinkle pumpkin seeds on top and enjoy!

Serves 4

Nutrition Tip: Pumpkin seeds are a great source of protein.

Warm Greens

Ingredients
1 bunch of kale
½ white onion
1 clove garlic
½ cup arugula
Olive oil
Salt and pepper, to taste

Directions
1. Add olive oil to pan on medium heat.

2. Add chopped garlic and onion sauté for 1-2 minutes.

3. Chop kale and arugula and add to pan, sautéing until soft.

5. Add salt, pepper and more olive oil when finished cooking.

Serves 2-4

Cooking Tip: Olive oil is best used after cooking or on top of salads since it is not a high heat oil.

Nutrient-Dense Foods Can Help Boost Energy Levels All Day Long

Zucchini Patties

Ingredients
1 large zucchini, grated (about 1 cup)
1 organic egg
Sea salt
Pepper
¼ tsp cumin
¼ tsp chili flakes
Grass-fed butter

Directions
1. Melt some grass-fed butter in a pan on medium heat.

2. In small bowl, scramble egg and spices.

3. Add zucchini and mix well.

4. Make four little zucchini patties and place in hot pan.

5. Cook over medium-high heat, turning once to brown.

6. Sprinkle with a little sea salt and serve.

Serves 2-3

Cooking Tip: You can also use coconut oil instead of grass-fed butter.

Simple Crock Pot Beans

Ingredients
1-2 cups of any dry beans of your choice
Water
Salt, cumin, pepper to taste

Directions
1. Place beans in a crock pot.

2. Cover beans with filtered water.

3. Turn crock pot on high and cook for 4-6 hrs- can cook on low for longer depending on your crock pot settings.

4. After beans are soft and cooked add salt, cumin, and pepper.

Cashew Cream

This recipe is by Dr. Bria Iacini, D.C. and Dr. Matthew Mutch, D.C. www.soulshinechiro.com

This recipe requires a long soaking period for the cashews. The more patience you have, the better your results will be.

Ingredients
⅔ cup raw & unsalted cashews
1 tsp ground cumin
6 tbsp freshly squeezed lime juice (3-4 medium limes)
¼ cup water
2 tsp sea salt

Directions

1. Soak the raw & unsalted cashews in room temperature water and cover for at least two hours or up to six hours (the longer soaking time yields better results). After soaking, drain excess water and add cashew nuts and place in blender.

2. Add cumin, lime juice, and HALF of the water to the blender. Start to blend the mixture on a low setting and gently increase the speed. If you notice that the mixture is too thick to mix, start to add the remainder of the water to dilute the cream. Blend for about one minute or until the mixture appears creamy.

3. Scoop into a serving dish and serve with your choice of main dish!

Easy Fried Rice
This recipe is by Mike Hudgens

Ingredients
1-2 cups rice (precooked)
2 eggs
3 tablespoons olive oil
¼ cup chopped onion
¼ cup diced organic carrot
1-2 cloves diced garlic
1-2 tablespoons tamari soy sauce
Add salt and pepper to taste

Directions
1. Add olive oil, garlic, onion and carrot into sauté pan on stove over med/high heat.

2. Cook until onions are translucent.

3. Add cooked rice and soy sauce and cook for approximately 5 minutes.

4. In a separate pan scramble the eggs.

5. Add eggs to rice mixture and stir while cooking for another 1-2 minutes.

6. Serve and enjoy!!

Tips: This is a perfect quick side dish or meal you can do with leftover rice. Our family even loves it for breakfast! You can make it "higher protein" by adding some cooked chicken to it.

Balance - Nourish - Inspire
The Simple Way...

Chapter 6: Simple Salads and Soups

Arugula Tomato Salad

Ingredients
1 bunch washed arugula
1 large organic tomato chopped
¼ cup sprouted pumpkin seeds
2 tbsp crumbled goat cheese

Dressing
2 tbsp olive oil
4 tbsp balsamic vinegar
¼ tsp sea salt
Pepper to taste
¼ tsp red pepper flakes

Directions
1. Combine all ingredients together for salad.

2. Make dressing and pour over salad.

Serves 2-4

Wash greens and make dressing ahead of time so this amazing salad can be made in 5 minutes!

Avocado Tomato and Cucumber Salad

Ingredients
1 ripe avocado, peeled and cut into cubes
1 ripe large organic tomato, chopped
1 peeled organic cucumber, chopped
¼ cup olive oil
2 tsp apple cider vinegar
Sea salt and pepper, to taste

Directions
1. Add all ingredients into medium bowl and mix well.

2. Serve alone or on a bed of organic mixed greens.

Serves 2-4

Cooking Tip: Add some feta or goat cheese to this easy salad!

Black Bean Salad

Ingredients
1 can BPA-free black beans, or soak 1 cup dried black beans for 12-18 hours, then drain and cook
¼ cup of cilantro
¼ cup of diced tomatoes
1 small cucumber, diced
¼ cup feta or goat cheese (optional)
1 tbsp of olive oil
Sea salt and pepper, to taste

Directions
1. Combine all ingredients in a medium size bowl.

2. Stir and enjoy!

Serves 4

Cooking Tip: Eat alone or with veggies or crackers or roll it up in a rice tortilla!

Easy Chicken Salad

Ingredients
1 cup cooked chicken chopped
2 stalks organic celery, chopped
Small handful of chopped red onion
2 tsp Dijon mustard
¼ cup vegan mayonnaise
Salt and pepper, to taste
Butter or Romaine lettuce leaves

Directions
1. Mix all the above ingredients together and serve over butter lettuce or romaine.

Serves 2-4

Cooking Tip: You can also use this chicken salad as a dip and serve with rice crackers or on top of rice cakes.

Creamy Broccoli Parsnip Soup

Ingredients
2 broccoli crowns
½ medium chopped white onion
2 chopped parsnips
1 can BPA-free coconut milk
½ cup vegetable or chicken broth
Salt and pepper, to taste
¼ tsp red pepper flakes (optional)

Directions
1. Place coconut milk, broth, broccoli, parsnips and onion into medium sized pot over medium to high heat until it comes to a boil. Stir occasionally.

2. Add red pepper flakes and salt and pepper, to taste.

3. Reduce heat and cover for about 45 minutes, or until veggies are soft.

Serves 4-6

Cooking Tip: If soup is too thick, add more broth.

Nourishing Chicken Soup
This recipe is by Mike Hudgens.

Ingredients
2 pre-cooked organic chicken breasts
1 32 oz. carton of chicken broth
2 cups filtered water
2 organic sliced carrots
2 organic onions, minced
2 bunches of baby bok choy, chopped
½ bunch of organic kale, diced and shredded
3 medium gold organic potatoes, chopped
2 large zucchini, sliced
3 cloves garlic, chopped
1 tbsp chopped fresh ginger
2 tbsp olive oil
Sea Salt
Pepper
Dried basil
Red pepper flakes (optional)

Directions
1. Place large pot on stovetop, heat over medium heat.

2. Add olive oil and chicken to pot and sauté for 3-5 minutes.

3. Add broth and water and stir.

4. Add all veggies and seasonings, to taste.

5. Stir and cover for 30-35 minutes, or until veggies are soft.

Serves 6-8

Simple Miso Soup

Ingredients
1-2 tbsp miso paste
Hot water
Green onions

Directions
1. Place 1-2 tbsp of miso paste in bowl or cup.

2. Pour hot water over it and stir.

3. Add chopped green onions on top, if desired.

Miso Types
Miso comes in different types, including soy bean miso and garbanzo miso. Miso is available at Whole Foods Market or other natural food stores. You can also add miso to sandwiches as a spread!

Nutrition Tips: Miso is an amazing fermented superfood. Do not cook miso because it is alive and full of natural cultures. It is fine to pour hot or boiling water over it.

Cold Avocado Tomato Soup

This recipe was inspired by *Nourishing Connections Cookbook.*

Ingredients
2 ripe avocados, peeled and pits removed
1 cup organic tomatoes, chopped small
2 cups organic yogurt or kefir
1 cup cold water
1 tsp sea salt
½ tsp pepper
½ tsp red pepper flakes (optional)

Directions
1. Add all ingredients to a high-speed blender or food processor and blend until smooth.

2. Place in refrigerator until soup is cold and enjoy!

Makes 4-6 cups

Cooking Tip: You can also use this cold soup as a topping on pasta or steamed cauliflower.

Nutrition Tip: Avocados are nutrient-dense and full of "good for you" fats!

Vegetable Minestrone Soup
This recipe is by JoEllen DeNicola

Ingredients
1 cup cooked garbanzo beans
1 cup red kidney beans
1 cup brown rice or barley
8 cups vegetable broth
1 thumb-length kombu sea vegetable
1 medium to large orange, yellow or red bell peppers
1 medium yellow onion chopped
3 medium zucchini
4 kale leaves, cut into strips and then halved
2 cups shiitake mushrooms
2 cups tomatoes, chopped
2 cloves garlic
1 tsp oregano
3 tbsp tomato paste
1 tbsp each: chopped rosemary and thyme, or 1 tsp of each dried
1 bay leaf
1 tbsp red cooking sherry
Salt and pepper, to taste

Directions
1. Precook rice and beans if you are not using canned beans. Add the kombu while cooking the rice and beans. (Remove the kombu prior to serving.)

2. In a stock pot, sauté the onions in olive oil over medium-low heat until translucent. Add the wine, garlic and red peppers, cook on low for 3 minutes.

3. Prepare the other vegetables, chopping or slicing as needed.

4. Add all the vegetables to the onions with the herbs and the broth. Add the beans and rice.

4. Bring to a boil and then reduce the heat until the flavors mingle, about 30-40 minutes. Season to taste with salt and pepper.

Serves 4-6

Nutrition Tips: This full meal offers all the necessary protein plus the nutrient rich qualities of the broth, vegetables, mushrooms and spices.

Shiitake mushrooms support the immune system and detoxify unwanted toxins from the system.

Kale is a cancer-fighting vegetable. It clears and cleans the system with its rich chlorophyll content.

Cooking Tip: This wholesome dish can be served with grated parmesan cheese.

Lentil, Coconut and Sweet Potato Soup

Ingredients
1 cup lentils
2 organic carrots, chopped
1 medium peeled sweet potato
1 can BPA-free coconut milk
½ cup water
Sea salt and pepper, to taste
¼ tsp turmeric
¼ tsp cumin
¼ tsp red pepper flakes

Directions
1. Place lentils, water and coconut milk in medium saucepan

2. Cook on high and reduce to medium-low heat after soup starts to boil.

3. Add all other ingredients, including spices. Stir and cover. Cook soup for 1 hour, or until veggies are soft. If soup is too thick, add more water.

Makes 4-5 cups

Cooking Tip: Lentils are a great source of daily fiber!

Nutrition Tip: Remember to soak your lentils for 24 hours, then drain water and add fresh water before cooking. This will help remove the phytic acid coating on the lentils for better digestion!

Muffin Tin Salad Bar for Kids And Adults

You will be creating a mini salad bar using a muffin pan. Kids love to help and create in the kitchen. This is a perfect way to make their **very own** personal salads. They get to choose what they want on their salad and create a RAINBOW on their plate at the same time!

You will need:
12 piece muffin tin
Lots of:
- Organic cherry tomatoes
- Chopped cucumbers
- Chopped organic carrots
- Chopped organic celery
- Goat cheese, feta or regular organic cheese cut in chunks
- Black or green olives
- Organic fresh blueberries

Washed mixed greens salad mix, or whatever type of lettuce your kids like.

Directions
1. Fill the muffin tins with whatever veggies your kids enjoy and put a few in there that they can try.

2. Place some mixed greens on kids' plates. Then, let them decorate a rainbow of color on their salad plate by using the veggies/fruits in the muffin pan. As the salad making is happing, take this time to talk about the veggies.

Some questions to ask kids when making salad:
- ✓ Where does this veggie grow?
- ✓ What color is this veggie?
- ✓ Why is it good for us?

Warm Sweet Potato Salad

Ingredients
1 bunch of washed organic mixed greens
Handful pumpkin seeds
Olive oil, for cooking sweet potatoes
Balsamic vinegar
Lemon
2 tbsp crumbled feta or goat cheese
2 medium sweet potatoes
Sea salt
Pepper
Dressing (see recipe, below)

Dressing:
¼ cup olive oil
3 tbsp balsamic vinegar or apple cider vinegar
1 tbsp fresh lemon
Salt and pepper to taste

Directions
1. Preheat oven to 375°F.

2. Peel, wash and place chopped sweet potatoes on a baking sheet.

3. Drizzle and lightly coat all sweet potatoes with olive oil.

4. Cook for approximately 45 minutes to 1 hour, or until soft.

5. Mix greens, pumpkin seeds, salt and pepper together in medium bowl.

6. Place warm cooked sweet potatoes and crumbled feta on top and enjoy!

Serves 2-4

Watermelon, Blueberry and Coconut Salad

No dressing is needed for this sweet salad!

Ingredients
2 cups seedless watermelon, chopped
1 cup organic blueberries
¼ cup shredded coconut

Directions
1. Mix all together and enjoy!

Serves 4

Entertaining Tip: This is the perfect 4th of July festive salad - red, white and blue!

Nutrition Tips: Blueberries are packed full of antioxidants.

Coconut is full of good-for-you fats.

Cucumber Chickpea Salad
This recipe is by JoEllen DeNicola

Ingredients:
2 medium cucumbers
½ cup chickpeas, cooked and cooled or canned
2 tbsp goji berries
½ cup chopped mint
1 cup plain goat kefir
Borage flowers, for garnish

1. Cut the cucumbers into rounds, about ¼ inch thick.

2. Add the mint to the kefir and mix well. Pour over the cucumbers, chickpeas and goji berries.

3. Garnish with borage flowers for that sparkling blue touch.

Serves 4

Kitchen Sink Salad

Ingredients
Chopped lettuce
Chopped carrots
Chopped tomato
Chopped broccoli
Chopped cucumbers
Chopped mushrooms
Pumpkin seeds
Sesame seeds
Sea salt and pepper, to taste

Directions
1. Place all above ingredients in a big bowl.

2. Toss with olive oil, balsamic vinegar, salt and pepper and enjoy.

Serves 2-4

Cooking Tip: You can add anything you want to the Kitchen Sink Salad. This is a great way to use up your veggies in the fridge before they go bad!

Amazing and Colorful Salad
Eat A Rainbow Of Color

Liver Love Salad
A salad that is nourishing for your liver

Ingredients
2 cups salad mix, or any lettuce you choose
A handful of pea shoots
A handful of sprouts or sprouted seeds
Some shredded beets/carrots
Shredded cabbage
A handful of pumpkin seeds

Lemon Olive Oil Dressing
Juice from a whole lemon
2-3 tbsp of olive oil (more if you want a less acidic taste)
Salt and pepper, to taste
½ tsp of fresh or dried rosemary
½ tsp of fresh or dried thyme

Directions
1. Combine liquid ingredients and herbs in a small bowl.

2. Pour dressing over salad and enjoy!

Serves 4

Nutrition Tip: This is a great salad to detox your liver health!

Quick Quinoa Salad

Ingredients
1 cup quinoa
2 cups water or broth
½ cup dried cranberries
1 medium size leek
¼ cup organic olive oil
¼ cup chia seeds
½ cup goat cheese
¼ tsp cumin
¼ tsp salt
¼ tsp pepper

Directions
1. Soak quinoa for at least 1 hour, but best soaked overnight.

2. Rinse and drain quinoa. Add 2 cups of water or broth.

3. Cook on high until boiling, then reduce heat to simmer for 10-15 minutes, or until fluffy.

4. After quinoa is cooked, set it aside to cool slightly in a glass bowl.

5. Add all other ingredients and stir.

Serves 4-6

Nutrition Tips: Quinoa is a gluten-free nourishing grain. It is high in protein and has a nutty flavor.

Cranberries are a great source of antioxidants and add a refreshing sweetness.

Simple Raw Kale Salad

Ingredients
½ cup extra virgin olive oil
¼ cup lemon juice
½ tsp coarse salt
Pinch red pepper flakes
2 bunches washed kale, ribs removed and leaves sliced into ¼-inch shreds

Directions
1. In a large bowl, whisk together oil, lemon juice, salt, and pepper flakes. Add kale and toss to coat.

2. Let sit at room temperature for 10 to 30 minutes.

3. You can also massage kale, oil, lemon, salt and pepper flakes to make the kale softer.

Serves 6

Nutrition Tip: Kale is a superfood. It is packed with lots of vitamins and minerals!

Keep it exciting!

Chapter 7: Delicious Dinner

15-Minute Meal: Kale and Sausage
This recipe is by Katja Heino with *Savory Lotus* (www.savorylotus.com).

Ingredients
1 bunch kale, chopped into thin ribbons
3-4 sausages
1 tbsp coconut aminos (a healthy soy sauce alternative)
1 tsp coconut oil, butter or ghee

Directions
1. Steam kale for 8-10 minutes. Remove from heat and toss with coconut aminos.

2. Meanwhile, chop sausage into bite-sized pieces and sauté in butter/ghee until thoroughly browned and thoroughly cooked.

3. Remove sausages from heat and add cooked kale.

4. Mix to combine and serve!

Serves 4

Cooking Tip: Katja recommends using organic and sustainable sausage, if possible. Chicken apple sausage is especially good in this recipe, but any savory flavor will work!

Amy's Healthy Taco Salad

Ingredients
1-2 pounds of ground turkey or chicken
1 can of BPA-free beans
1 cup chopped lettuce
1 cup chopped tomatoes
½ cup salsa
½ cup chopped cilantro
½ cup chopped onion
Salt, pepper, cumin, turmeric and red chili flakes, to taste

Directions
1. Cook up 1-2 pounds of ground turkey or ground chicken on stovetop.

2. Add spices to the ground meat while cooking.

3. Place ground turkey on a bed of lettuce greens.

4. Top with beans, tomato, salsa, cilantro and onion. Serve with some organic blue corn tortilla chips.

Serves 4

Cooking Tip: Have veggies and lettuce washed ahead of time to make this fast meal even faster!

Amy's Turkey Chili

Ingredients
2 pounds ground turkey or chicken
1-2 cans kidney beans (or any kind of beans you like)
1 can stewed tomatoes
1 tsp cumin
1 tsp turmeric
1 tsp nutmeg
1 tbsp cinnamon
½ cup water
Salt and pepper, to taste

Directions
1. Place ground turkey in large Dutch oven. Salt and pepper the turkey while cooking to give it flavor. Cook until done.

2. Add in beans, stewed tomatoes and spices.

3. Let cook on low heat for a few hours.

Serves 4

Cooking Tip: If you're in a rush, just make sure the ground turkey is fully cooked and add in the rest of the ingredients. Cook all together for 30 minutes and serve.

Spinach Cilantro Turkey Burgers

This recipe is by Katja Heino with *Savory Lotus*
(www.savorylotus.com).

Ingredients
1 pound organic ground turkey (dark meat)
½ small onion, finely chopped
2 handfuls of baby spinach, washed and chopped
½ tsp Herbamare seasoning
½ tsp Celtic sea salt
¼ cup fresh cilantro, finely chopped
1 tbsp ghee or butter for cooking

Optional Toppings:
Avocado
Homemade pickles
Lettuce
Caramelized onions

Directions
1. In a large bowl, combine ground turkey and next five ingredients and mix well.

2. Form into five patties.

3. Melt ghee or butter in a skillet on medium heat.

4. Cook patties until nice and brown, flipping a couple of times. This usually takes about 15 minutes.

5. Serve over a bed of lettuce. Top with caramelized onions, avocado and other toppings of your choice.

Makes 5 burgers

Simple Frittata

Ingredients
6 eggs
1 ounce of Parmesan grated
1 tsp grass fed butter
½ cup chopped arugula
½ cup chopped chicken
½ cup chopped red bell pepper
Salt and pepper, to taste

Directions
1. Preheat oven to broil setting.

2. In a medium bowl using a fork blend together eggs, Parmesan, pepper and salt.

3. Heat pan over medium heat and add butter. Add arugula and chicken, and sauté for 3 minutes. Pour egg mixture into pan and cook for 4-5 minutes, or until mixture has begun to set.

4. Place pan into oven and broil for 3-4 more minutes, or until brown and fluffy.

Serves 6

Cooking Tip: Sprinkle chopped parsley, goat cheese and red pepper flakes on top of the frittata after it is cooked to add a little KICK to this simple dish!

Simple Baked Salmon

Ingredients
4 medium pieces of fresh wild salmon
Salt and pepper, to taste
1 tsp olive oil
1 lemon

Directions
1. Preheat oven to 375°F.

2. Cut lemon into thin slices.

3. Place salmon pieces in a baking dish and add salt, pepper, olive oil and lemon slices on top.

4. Bake for 20-30 minutes, or until cooked.

Serves 4-6

Nutrition Tips: Salmon is a superfood! It is packed full of Omega-3's in every bite. Please only buy wild salmon, NOT farmed salmon. Buy at local fish markets or vitalchoice.com.

Simple Veggie Stir Fry

Ingredients
1 cup organic brown rice
1 cup shredded organic carrots
1 cup chopped organic kale
½ cup chopped white onion
1 cup chopped organic broccoli
1 cup chopped organic bok choy
¼ cup chopped organic red bell pepper
½ cup chopped purple cabbage
3 tbsp grape seed oil- or coconut oil
¼ tsp red pepper flakes
1 tsp cumin
1 tsp turmeric
Salt and pepper, to taste

Directions
1. Soak rice for 24 hours.

2. Drain rice and add 2 cups fresh water to 1 cup of rice.

3. Cook for 35-45 minutes, or until water is absorbed and set aside.

4. Heat another pan over medium to medium-high heat. Add grapeseed oil.

5. Add all ingredients except rice and sauté until veggies turn bright in color and are a bit soft. Serve over the rice.

Serves 4-6

Nutrition Tips: You can add some olive oil after cooking.

Olive oil is not a high heat oil, so it is best used over food after cooking. Coconut oil and grapeseed oil are high heat oils.

Stuffed Peppers
This recipe is by JoEllen DeNicola.

Ingredients
4 medium to large orange, yellow or red bell peppers
1 cup millet
1 medium yellow onion chopped
2 tbsp olive oil
4 kale leaves, cut into strips and then halved
1 cup cooked garbanzo beans
½ currants or cranberries
2 tbsp fresh chopped rosemary
1 tbsp dry cooking sherry
Salt and pepper, to taste

Directions
1. Preheat oven to 375°F then toast the millet in a saucepan until you can smell a pleasant aroma. Add 2 cups of water and cook for 20 minutes or until fluffy. Remove and cool on a cookie sheet.

3. Cut the bell peppers in half, removing the seeds. Place them in a steamer and steam them for five minutes. Place them into a baking dish with the open sides up.

4. While the onions steam, sauté the chopped yellow onions in olive oil over medium heat until translucent, about 8 minutes.

5. Remove kale leaves from the stems. Cut kale leaves into strips and then in half, add to sautéed onions, adding the rosemary, cooking sherry, salt and pepper. Cook 5 more mins.

6. Combine the onions, kale, garbanzo beans, currants, and millet; taste to see if you need to add salt or pepper. Spoon filling into the prepared bell peppers.

7. Cover and bake for 25 minutes, or until very hot.

Serves 4

Grass-Fed Beef "Crock Pot" Stew

Ingredients
1½ pounds grass-fed stew meat
3 organic carrots, chopped
2 organic celery stalks, chopped
2 cloves garlic, chopped
1 turnip, chopped
1 parsnip, chopped
2 tsp sea salt
1 tsp pepper
1 tsp cumin
½ tsp turmeric
2-3 cups water or broth
1 tsp red pepper flakes- optional

Directions
1. Place all above ingredients into a crock pot and turn on high until cooked, approximately 4-6 hours. You can also cook all day on low.

Serves 4-6

Cooking Tips: Red or yellow organic potatoes can be used in place of root veggies.

Slow cookers are the best, and perfect for the busy family. Search online for other easy slow cooker recipes for a meal that will be ready when you get home from a busy day!

Roasted Chicken
This recipe is by Mike Hudgens.

Ingredients
1 whole organic chicken, approximately 4 pounds
3 organic celery stalks
3 large organic carrots
5 medium organic red or gold potatoes
4 cloves of garlic
½ cup water or broth

Seasoning suggestions:
Rosemary
Thyme
Sage
Salt
Pepper

Directions
1. Preheat oven to 375°F.

2. Chop all vegetables into 3-inch pieces.

3. Arrange celery on bottom of a Dutch oven. Place chicken on top of celery.

4. Arrange other vegetables around whole chicken and add liquid or broth.

5. Add seasonings and cover with lid.

6. Cook for approximately 1½ hours or until fully cooked.

Serves 6

Stuffed Acorn Squash
This recipe is by JoEllen DeNicola

Ingredients
4 acorn squash, medium in size
1 cup millet, soaked overnight and rinsed
1 cup vegetable or chicken broth
2 tbsp olive oil
¼ cup red onion, finely chopped
¼ cup sweet peppers, chopped into small cubes
¼ cup celery, finely chopped
¼ cup carrots, finely chopped
1 tsp fresh rosemary
1 tsp fresh thyme
1 tsp fresh parsley
Salt and pepper, to taste
1 cup arame, crunched up and soaked if you like
Parmesan cheese, grated (optional)

Directions
5. Cut the top third off the acorn squash and remove the seeds.

6. Place in a glass baking dish with enough water on the bottom to cover the dish.

7. Bring the broth to a boil. Add the millet and simmer for 15-20 minutes.

8. While the millet simmers, over a medium heat sauté the red onions until they are clear.

9. Add all the vegetables and sauté for 5-7 minutes.

10. Turn off the heat and mix in the herbs. Mix in the arame.

11. Add the sautéed vegetables to the cooked grains and spoon them into the center of the acorn squash.

12. Sprinkle Gomasio or a grated cheese over the top and add pat of butter.

13. Cover with foil and bake.

Serves 3-4

Fun Fish Tacos

Ingredients
2 pieces of white fish - cod or tilapia
½ cup chopped cilantro
½ cup chopped white onion
½ cup chopped organic tomatoes
1 lime
6-8 organic corn tortillas
Olive oil
Salt and pepper, to taste

Directions
1. Salt fish on both sides.

2. Place a bit of olive oil in pan on medium heat.

3. Place fish in hot pan and grill on one side for 5 minutes (less if fish is thin).

4. Flip and grill on the other side for 1-3 minutes, or until fully cooked. Fish will flake a bit when it is cooked.

5. Place all above ingredients in corn tortillas and top with fresh lime juice.

Serves 4-6

Cooking Tip: Serve with organic yogurt for extra "yumminess" and nutrition!

Turkey Meatballs

Ingredients
¾ pound of ground turkey
1 organic egg, beaten
2 tsp grapeseed oil
1 tsp Himalayan sea salt
½ white onion, finely chopped
1 tsp flax meal
1 piece gluten-free bread, crumbled
1 clove garlic, finely chopped

Directions
1. Preheat oven to 400°F.

2. Mix all ingredients together and roll into little balls.

3. Place rolled balls onto a parchment paper-lined baking sheet.

4. Bake for 30 minutes or until golden brown.

Makes approximately 20 meatballs

Nutrition Tip: Grapeseed oil is a great choice for a high heat oil.

Quick Carne Asada, Arugula and Rice

Ingredients

½ pound of grass-fed carne asada meat
1 cup organic raw arugula
1 cup organic white basmati rice - precooked makes it easier!
Salt and pepper

Directions

1. Cook carne asada meat on stove top with a little butter or olive oil for 3-5 minutes on each side (cook longer if you like it well done). This meat cooks fast since it is so thin.

2. Chop up meat and place it on top of cooked rice, then put the arugula on top of that for a beautiful presentation.

3. Add salt, pepper and other spices and enjoy!

Quick Tip: This is an easy 5-10 minute meal for dinner with protein, carbs and veggies! You can add any veggies to this that you would like including avocado for some healthy fats.

Quick Crock Pot Chicken and Beans

Ingredients
3-4 boneless skinless organic chicken breasts
1 can organic tomatoes with sauce
½ cup filtered water - optional if you want it more "saucey"
1 can white beans, drained and rinsed
1 zucchini, chopped
1 organic bell pepper, chopped
Basil, cumin, salt and pepper
Add any spices you want – basil, cilantro, pepper, chili flakes etc.

Directions
1. Place chicken in crock pot.

2. Place zucchini, bell pepper, beans, spices and tomatoes over the chicken evenly. Add ½ cup water on top. Add more water if you want more liquid.

3. Cook on low for 6-8 hours.

Make sure to drink eight to ten big glasses of filtered water each day. Proper hydration is very important for your overall health and wellness.

Adding lemon and sea salt to your water is a simple and fresh way to get electrolytes into your body!

Chapter 8: Nourishing Treats

Almond Butter Coconut Dates

Ingredients
6 pitted dates
¼ cup almond butter or cashew butter
¼ cup of shredded coconut
Himalayan salt

Directions
1. Fill each pitted date with almond butter.

2. Sprinkle salt and shredded coconut on top.

3. Enjoy right away or store in the refrigerator for up to 3 days.

Makes 6

Nutrition Tip: Dates are an alkaline food and can help reduce inflammation in the body.

Almond Chocolate Bites

This recipe was inspired by a *Savory Lotus* recipe "Flowerless Almond Chocolate Chip Cookies." See www.savorylotus.com for more amazing recipes.

Ingredients

1 cup almond butter
1 egg
¼ cup honey
½ cup shredded almonds
½ cup shredded coconut
¼ tsp sea salt
2 squares of dark chocolate, chopped
½ tsp baking soda
2 tsp cacao powder

Directions

1. Preheat oven to 350°F.

2. Mix almond butter and honey in a large bowl until smooth. Add in shredded coconut, almonds, baking soda and chocolate and mix together.

3. Using a spoon, form into balls and place on a parchment-lined baking sheet.

4. Bake for 10 minutes or until golden brown. Let cool.

Serves 20

Important Reminder: Only children over 1 year of age should consume honey as infants are at risk of botulism.

Cashew Butter Crumble

Ingredients
3 tbsp cashew butter
2 tbsp coconut oil
½ cup organic rolled oats
½ cup organic rice puffed cereal
¼ cup chia seeds
¼ cup dried cranberries
¼ tsp cardamom
¼ tsp cinnamon

Directions
1. Heat cashew butter, coconut, cardamom and cinnamon on medium heat on stove until melted. Be careful not to let it burn!

2. After above is melted, turn off heat and add in oats, rice cereal, chia seeds, and cranberries. Stir together.

3. Let crumbly mixture cool and then place in Mason jar.

Serves 6

Cooking Tip: This crumble is great on top of yogurt or by itself with some almond milk.

Avocado Chocolate Pudding

Ingredients
1 avocado
1 tbsp cacao powder
1 tsp honey
A pinch of cinnamon

Directions
1. Peel avocado.

2. Place all ingredients in blender.

3. Blend until smooth and enjoy.

Cooking Tips: You can add chopped bananas and walnuts to this healthy pudding for some extra sweetness and crunch.

Sprinkle cayenne pepper on top for a little spice!

Banana Fig Drop Cookies

This recipe was inspired by the *Nourishing Connections Cookbook.*

Ingredients
2 bananas, mashed
1 cup rolled oats
⅔ cup rice flower
¼ tsp baking soda
¼ cup melted coconut oil
¼ sea salt
½ tsp cinnamon
¼ tsp cardamom
⅓ cup mashed figs, skins removed

Directions
1. Preheat oven to 350°F.

2. Mix all above ingredients together.

3. Using a tablespoon, drop dough on a parchment-lined baking sheet.

4. Bake 15 minutes or until golden brown on bottom.

Makes about 15-20 cookies

Cooking Tip: When figs are not in season, you can use dried cranberries, finely chopped kale or bits of dried apricots.

Date Coconut Truffles

Ingredients
1 cup almond butter
1 cup pitted dates
1 cup dried cranberries
1 tsp cinnamon
¼ tsp cardamom
1 cup shredded coconut
Cinnamon

Directions
1. Place all ingredients through cardamom in food processor.

2. Pulse until the mixture forms a ball.

3. Mix coconut and cinnamon in a small bowl.

4. Roll almond butter mixture into little balls. Roll in coconut and cinnamon mixture.

5. Place in fridge for 20-30 minutes to harden a bit and enjoy.

Makes about 20 truffles

Nutrition Tip: Coconut is packed full of healthy fats.

Heavenly Sweet Potato Pudding

This recipe is by Katja Heino with Savory Lotus (www.savorylotus.com) and is inspired by Mollie Katzen's Sunlight Café.

Ingredients

1½ cups cooked, mashed yam
½ tsp Celtic sea salt
¼ tsp allspice
Pinch of ground cloves
1¼ cup coconut milk
¼ cup honey
¼ tsp cinnamon
¼ tsp ground ginger
5 eggs, beaten
2 tsp vanilla extract
Coconut oil, butter, or ghee for oiling ramekins

Optional garnish:

Unsweetened shredded coconut, coconut sugar and cinnamon

1. Fill a large baking pan halfway with water and place into oven on the center rack. Preheat oven to 350°F.

2. Lightly oil 6 ramekins.

3. Combine mashed yams and honey in a large bowl. Add salt and spices. Mix well to combine. Stir in the beaten eggs and mix again until well combined. Pour in coconut milk and vanilla. Stir again. *If using optional garnish, combine shredded coconut, coconut sugar and cinnamon in a small bowl. Set aside.*

4. Spoon mixture into oiled ramekins, dividing it equally among the 6 cups. Sprinkle with optional garnish if desired. Carefully place ramekins into the baking pan with hot water in the oven.

5. Bake for 35-40 minutes, until pudding is solid and a toothpick comes out clean. It's okay if the center is a bit soft as it will continue to cook after coming out of oven. Very carefully remove baking pan from oven. Then use kitchen tongs to remove individual ramekins from the pan.

6. Allow to cool completely before serving. This pudding tastes the best at room temperature or cold out of the fridge. Store leftovers in refrigerator, tightly covered.

Serves 6

Chia Pudding

Ingredients
1 cup water or nut milk
¼ cup chia seeds
¼ tsp cinnamon
¼ tsp cardamom

Directions
1. Combine water or nut milk with chia seeds in a Mason jar.

2. Cover and shake well.

3. Place in refrigerator overnight or at least 6 hours.

Serves 4

Nutrition Tip: Use a scoop of chia pudding in your smoothies, on toast, in oatmeal, or just eat a spoonful! Chia seeds are high in Omega-3's and are very hydrating for the body.

Grain-Free Easy Brownies

Ingredients
1 cup blanched almond flour
¼ tsp sea salt
¼ tsp baking soda
⅓ cup raw cacao powder
½ cup melted coconut oil
3 organic eggs
1 tsp vanilla extract

Directions
1. Preheat oven to 350°F and grease a mini muffin pan.

2. Add all dry ingredients to a medium bowl and stir to combine.

3. In a small bowl, beat eggs, then add melted coconut oil and the rest of the wet ingredients. Mix until smooth.

4. Pour wet ingredients into dry and stir.

5. Spoon mixture into greased mini muffin pans and cook for approximately 15 minutes.

Makes 24 mini muffin brownies

Figs with Spicy Honey Drizzle

This is a perfect simple treat for a picnic or to take to a party. So simple and yummy!

Ingredients
8 figs
¼ cup honey
2 tsp red pepper flakes
⅓ cup crumbled goat cheese

Directions
1. Slice figs in half.

2. Mix red pepper flakes and honey in a small bowl.

3. Place figs and goat cheese on plate.

4. When ready to eat, place a small amount of goat cheese on each fig, drizzle with honey mixture and enjoy!

Serves 4-6

Berry Gummy Treats

This recipe is by Katja Heino with *Savory Lotus*
(www.savorylotus.com)

Ingredients
1½ cups berries, fresh or frozen (any combo of strawberries, blueberries, raspberries, or blackberries)
1 cup water
4 tbsp fresh lemon juice
2-3 tbsp honey
4 tbsp grass-fed gelatin

Directions
1. Combine water and berries in a small pot on the stove. Gently bring to a simmer and cook for 3-4 minutes to soften berries. Remove from heat and allow to cool for 5 minutes.

2. Use an immersion blender to puree mixture until smooth. A blender will work but be careful not to burn yourself.

3. Stir in honey until completely dissolved. Then vigorously whisk in gelatin one tablespoon at a time (to prevent clumping).

4. Pour into an 8x8-inch glass baking dish or any silicone molds that you may have. Place in fridge for at least an hour to set. Cut into desired sized cubes or remove from molds.

Makes 20-30 squares

Lemon Berry Tart
This recipe is by JoEllen DeNicola

Ingredients
Almond Crust:
6½ cups almonds, soaked overnight and drained
¾ cup pitted Medjool dates, drained and quartered – soak if they are not soft
6 tbsp of your favorite nut or coconut butter
6 tsp almond extract
¾ tsp cinnamon
Pinch of sea salt

Cashew Cream Filling:
6 cup cashews, soaked overnight and drained
6 pitted Medjool dates, soaked for 20 minutes, drained and chopped
½ cup lemon juice, or 6 drops of lemon essential oil

Berry Topping:
2 cups blueberries, raspberries or blackberries
1 cup strawberries, sliced

Directions
1. Combine the crust ingredients in a food processor. Using an "S" blade, pulse then process until smooth. Press into a tart pan.

2. Place the filling ingredients into the food processor and, using the "S" blade, process until creamy and smooth.

3. Pour the filling into the crust.

4. Place the berries onto the filling, creating a beautiful pie. Refrigerate for 3-4 hours and serve.

Serves 4-6

Nutrition Tips: This raw tart is a gem! Berries are anti-inflammatory, support the nervous system and provide vitamins. The pie is naturally sweet and filling, too. Plus, it is a beautiful treat and is gluten-free.

Cooking Tips: You can use orange juice instead of lemon juice for the filling.

Add almond extract to the filling.

Non-Dairy Fruity Ice Cream

Ingredients
2 frozen bananas
½ cup fresh organic blueberries
½ cup fresh raspberries
½ tsp cinnamon
3 tbsp coconut milk

Directions
1. Blend bananas, blueberries, raspberries and coconut milk in a food processor or high-speed blender.

2. Scoop into little bowls and garnish with cinnamon.

Serves 2-4

Cooking Tips: Optional garnish: raw cacao powder or shredded bits of 70% dark chocolate.

You can freeze right after making or enjoy immediately!

Amazing Raw Apple " Pie"

Ingredients
2 medium red or green organic apples
2-4 tbsp of almond butter, or any nut butter
1 tsp cinnamon
¼ tsp cardamom - optional
Optional: organic whole fat plain or Greek yogurt

Directions
1. Slice apples vertically so they are flat little circles.

2. Place apples on a plate.

3. Spread some almond butter evenly on each apple slice.

4. Top with cinnamon and optional yogurt and enjoy!

Fun Tip: This is a great easy fun dessert or snack to make with kids. Loaded with fiber and protein!

Baked Banana "Pie"

Ingredients
1-2 bananas
1 tbsp almond butter or cashew butter
¼ tsp cinnamon
dash of sea salt
Organic full fat yogurt

Optional toppings- chocolate chips, cardamom, nutmeg, slivered almonds, flax meal or pumpkin seeds

Directions
1. Slice bananas down the middle and fill with almond butter, cinnamon and salt.

2. Place them in an oven safe baking dish.

3. Bake for 15 minutes at 375°F.

4. Let cool for a couple minutes and top with almond butter, cinnamon, salt and a dollop of yogurt (optional) and enjoy!

Tips: This is an easy nourishing dessert that kids love to help prepare. Bananas are full of potassium and almond butter is loaded with protein! Enjoy this "healthier" dessert with your family.

Coconut Freezer Pops
This recipe is by Katja Heino with *Savory Lotus*
(www.savorylotus.com)

Ingredients
2 cups homemade coconut milk (or 1 can)
2-3 tbsp honey or maple syrup (use less if needed)
1½ cups berries or chopped fruit, fresh or frozen

Directions
1. Mix coconut and sweetener of choice together until well combined.

2. Stand popsicle holders upright and fill partially with berries or chopped fruit.

3. Pour coconut milk mixture over fruit, gently jiggling popsicle holder to get milk to settle in and fill the holder.

4. Place in freezer until completely frozen. (Don't forget to put in the popsicle handles!)

Makes 6 large popsicles

Crazy Coconut Whipped Cream

Ingredients
2 cans full fat coconut milk
1 tsp honey
½ tsp cinnamon – optional

Directions
1. Place can of coconut milk in fridge for 6-12 hours (or overnight) or, for a shortcut, in the freezer for 1-2 hours.

2. Open can and scrape out only thick cream and place in mixing bowl. Discard watery coconut milk or use for smoothies later.

3. Add honey to cream mixture.

4. Use a high-speed mixer and blend the coconut cream for approximately 10 minutes on medium-high speed.

5. Refrigerate for a couple of hours and enjoy!

Cooking Tip: the trick making this a success is to make sure your coconut cream is not watery. So you can use 1-2 cans of coconut milk depending on how much you want to make…Just remember to only use the thick cream not the watery milk inside the can.

Flourless Almond Chocolate Chip Cookies

This recipe is by Katja Heino with *Savory Lotus*
(www.savorylotus.com)

Ingredients
1 cup almond butter
¼ cup raw honey
1 egg
½ cup sliced almonds
½ cup chocolate chips
¼ cup shredded coconut, unsweetened
½ tsp unrefined sea salt
½ tsp baking soda

Directions
1. Preheat oven to 325° F.

2. Mix almond butter and honey in a large bowl until smooth.

3. Add egg, salt, shredded coconut, and baking soda and mix again.

4. Fold in chocolate chips and sliced almonds.

5. Using a tablespoon, form the dough into round balls and place on baking pan lined with parchment paper or silicone baking mat.

6. Press balls down slightly, depending on how thick you want your cookies.

7. Bake 8-11 minutes until cookies are golden brown.

8. Let cool completely before removing from pan (or cool for 15 minutes on baking pan then transfer to cooling rack).

Frozen Dark Chocolate Banana Bites

Ingredients
2-3 Bananas
½ cup dark chocolate chips or bar, broken into pieces
Handful shredded organic coconut flakes
Optional: Coarse sea salt, cinnamon, cardamom or cayenne pepper

Directions
1. Slice bananas and lay them on parchment paper on plate or baking pan.

2. Heat chocolate on low heat in a small pot until melted.

3. Drizzle chocolate on each banana slice.

4. Top with a little bit of shredded coconut on each slice on banana.

5. Add some optional toppings on if you desire.

6. Place in freezer until chocolate is bit hard (takes about an hour).

Fun tip: These are easy to make and kids love them! Great for summer months or anytime! Bananas have lots of potassium in them. Dark chocolate (over 70%) is rich in antioxidants and minerals. Enjoy!

Pumpkin Spice Donuts (Gluten-, Grain-, Nut- and Dairy-Free)

This recipe is by Katja Heino with *Savory Lotus* (www.savorylotus.com)

Ingredients

¼ cup coconut flour, sifted
½ tsp baking soda
½ tsp unrefined salt
1 tsp cinnamon powder
½ tsp ginger powder
½ tsp cardamom powder
⅛ tsp nutmeg
⅛ tsp clove
3 eggs
1 tbsp coconut oil, melted
1 tsp vanilla extract
¼ cup maple syrup
½ cup pumpkin puree
coconut oil for greasing donut pan
OPTIONAL for topping: ¼ cup coconut sugar and 1 tsp cinnamon powder

Directions

1. Preheat oven to 350° F and LIBERALLY grease donut pan.

2. Combine coconut flour, baking soda, salt, and spices in a large bowl. Set aside.

3. In another bowl, whisk together eggs, coconut oil, maple syrup, and vanilla extract. Add pumpkin puree and whisk again.

4. Add wet ingredients to the dry, mix until well incorporated, and allow to sit for a couple of minutes to let the coconut flour absorb.

5. Place the batter in a piping bag or a large Ziploc bag with the end cut off the end so there's about a ½-inch opening.

6. Fill each cavity in donut pan ¾ full. Give the pan a little shake or two to let the batter settle. (Do not overfill as they will be hard to remove from pan)

7. Bake for 18 minutes, or until toothpick inserted comes out clean and edges are just beginning to brown.

8. Remove from oven and allow to cool. Gently remove from donut pan and dip into optional cinnamon coconut sugar. (Combine coconut sugar and cinnamon in a shallow bowl. Dip each donut to cover).

Serves 6

Cooking Tips: For best results, dip the donuts in the cinnamon coconut sugar just before serving. Due to the nature of the coconut sugar, it will absorb the moisture from the donut and not be as visible.

Simple Sweet Potato "Pie"
Inspired by Lily Mazzarella

Ingredients
2 sweet potatoes
1 tbsp almond butter or sunflower seed butter
¼ tsp cinnamon
Optional: Crazy Coconut Whipped Cream (page 196)

Directions
1. Heat oven to 350° F.

2. Bake sweet potatoes with skin on at for about 45 minutes or until fork can slid through easily.

3. Slice into large rounds about ¼ inch thick.

4. Top with almond butter, cinnamon and whipped cream.

Serves 2

Fun Tip: This amazing dessert (or snack) is so simple and loaded with vitamins and protein. It really does taste like pie without all the work of making a pie from scratch.

Paleo Apple Pear Crisp

Ingredients
Filling:
3 organic apples, peeled and sliced thin
1 small organic pear, sliced thin
2 tsp fresh lemon juice
1 tsp cinnamon
Optional:
½ tsp cardamom
½ tsp ground nutmeg

Topping:
1¼ cups almond meal
half a stick of butter
1 tsp cinnamon
¼ tsp Himalayan or sea salt
a little melted butter to grease the pan

Directions
1. Heat oven to 350° F.
2. Mix all the apples/pears in a bowl and toss with lemon juice and cinnamon.
3. Make topping in separate bowl and mix together.
4. Grease the baking dish with melted butter (or coconut oil if avoiding dairy).
5. Place apples/pears in baking dish and add topping.
6. Bake for approximately 45 minutes or until apples are soft.
7. Top with Crazy Coconut Whipped Cream (page 196) if desired.

Tips: This is a wonderful dessert full of fiber and healing warming spices like cinnamon.

Chapter 9: Smoothies, Nut Milks and Drinks

Strawberry Chia Smoothie

Ingredients
1 cup coconut milk
¾ cup plain whole milk yogurt
½ cup frozen strawberries
1-2 pitted dates
2 tsp chia seeds
2 tsp flax meal

Directions
1. Place all above ingredients in blender and blend until smooth.

Nutrition Tip: Chia seeds are hydrating for the body and full of Omega-3's.

Homemade Almond Milk

Ingredients
1 cup raw almonds
3 cups filtered water
½ tsp vanilla (optional)
Pinch of cinnamon

Directions
1. Soak the almonds for 12-18 hours.

2. Blend almonds, water, vanilla, and cinnamon until almost smooth.

3. Strain the blended almond mixture using a strainer or cheese cloth.

Cooking Tip: Homemade raw almond milk will keep well in the refrigerator for three or four days

Nutrition Tip: Homemade almond milk has no added sugar. Enjoy pure nourishment!

Berry Protein Smoothie

Ingredients
1 cup frozen organic raspberries
½ tbsp chia seeds
1 tbsp almond butter
4 oz. coconut milk
½ of a banana
¼ cup shredded coconut
1 tsp of cacao nibs
¼ tsp cinnamon
Pinch of ground cardamom

Directions
1. Combine all ingredients together in a blender and blend until smooth.

2. Add a small amount of water to get desired consistency.

Nutrition Tip: Berries are lower on the glycemic index than most other fruits.

Making smoothies can be a Quick and Simple way to add Nourishment into your diet...

Date Avocado Smoothie

Ingredients
¾ cup coconut milk
¼ cup pitted dates
½ avocado
½ cup frozen blueberries
½ tsp cinnamon
¼ cup plain yogurt or kefir
1 tbsp protein powder (optional)

Directions
1. Blend all above ingredients together and enjoy!

2. Add ice for colder and thicker smoothie.

Nutrition Tip: This is a perfect morning smoothie packed with healthy fats, antioxidants and protein!

Homemade Hemp Milk

Ingredients
1 cup hemp seeds
Honey
Cinnamon
Vanilla

Directions
1. Soak 1 cup of hemp seeds for 2 hours.

2. Drain seeds.

3. Add drained hemp seeds and 3 cups water to blender.

4. Blend until smooth.

5. Filter the seeds through cheesecloth or a fine strainer.

6. You can add honey, cinnamon and vanilla or anything that sounds yummy.

Homemade Oat Milk

Ingredients
½ cup of rolled oats (not quick cook)
4 cups of filtered water
Cinnamon
Vanilla

Directions
1. Soak oats for 20 minutes. Drain water, add fresh water.

2. Blend up together in blender.

3. Strain oats with a fine strainer or cheesecloth.

4. Add cinnamon and vanilla to taste.

5. Drink and enjoy! Homemade oat milk will last two-three days in refrigerator in a glass container.

Nutrition Tips: Oats are so nourishing, great for the nervous system, and they calm the body. Oats are also a great source of non-dairy calcium.

Soaking oats (and all grains and legumes) helps remove the phytic acid coat that surrounds the oat. By soaking for even 20 minutes, this can help aid digestion and allow minerals and vitamins to be more accessible to the body.

Kale-Apple Smoothie

Ingredients
1 cup rice milk
½ cup chopped kale, ribs removed
½ of a banana
½ cup chopped apple
Juice from ½ fresh lemon

Directions
1. Place all above ingredients in a blender and blend until smooth.

Nutrition Tip: You can also use coconut milk, almond milk or kefir instead of rice milk for added nourishment.

Oat Milk Date Smoothie

Ingredients
1½ cups oat milk
½ cup pitted dates
½ tsp of cinnamon
½ tsp of nutmeg
Ice (optional)

Optional Additions:
½ of a banana
½ cup blueberries
1 tbsp flax meal
Handful of spinach
Some rice, hemp, or pea protein powder

Directions
1. Place all ingredients in blender and blend until smooth.

2. Add ice to make it cold and thick, if desired.

Easy Fresh Almond Milk Made Simple!

Pumpkin Coconut Smoothie

Ingredients
½ cup coconut milk
¼ cup pumpkin puree
¼ cup shredded coconut
1 pitted date
1 tsp cinnamon
¼ tsp nutmeg
½ of a banana
½ cup ice

Directions
1. Place all above ingredients in blender and blend until smooth.

Nutrition Tip: Add protein powder for extra quick protein.

Simple and Nourishing Green Juice
Use a juicer to make this nourishing juice!

Ingredients
1 medium organic cucumber (peel if not organic)
4-5 stalks of organic celery
1 organic apple or pear
A handful of organic curly parsley

Directions
1. Wash all veggies/fruits and cut into medium pieces to fit best in your juicer. Juice in the order listed above.

2. Make sure when juicing you juice more green veggies than fruit - I do 3 green veggies to 1 fruit.

Serves 4 small glasses

Nutritional Benefits of Juices
Celery juice
- ✓ A good source of magnesium, sodium and iron
- ✓ Quiets the nerves and may provide sound sleep
- ✓ Contains vitamin C

Parsley Juice
- ✓ Use only a bit (2 ounces or so) because it is highly concentrated
- ✓ An important cleansing herb
- ✓ Strongly alkaline
- ✓ Contains calcium, iron, potassium and magnesium

Cucumber Juice
- ✓ Cucumbers are very cooling for the digestive system
- ✓ Super refreshing

Apple Juice
- ✓ Full of fiber and vitamins

Nylah's Nourishing Tea

Ingredients
½ tsp dried nettle
½ tsp anise seed
1 tsp chamomile
8-12 oz. boiling water

Directions
Combine all herbs and water in a Mason jar (or tea pot). Cover and let steep for 10 minutes. I like to sweeten the tea with local honey and cinnamon.

Nutrition Tips: The health benefits of nettle include that it stimulates lymphatic function, helps with inflammation and allergies, and boosts nutrition and immunity. This tea contains iron, calcium, potassium and vitamin C.

- **Anise Seeds:** these seeds have a warming effect on digestion and upper respiratory tracks. Use as a natural decongestant.
- **Chamomile**: Relaxing and calming
- **Local honey:** honey is an overall health aid, contains antibacterial properties. **Buy local honey** to help prevent allergies and boost immunity. **Only give honey to babies over age 1.**
- **Add Cinnamon:** Cinnamon is a great warming spice, antia fungal, antibacterial, and great to use to prevent and ease the common cold.
- *The herbs are available at Oliver's, Rosemary's Garden or Whole Foods.*

Chapter 10: Resources and Pantry
Networking With Friends Made Simple!
Meet some of the most amazing practitioners and business owners that I respect & work with!

Local Resources Made Simple

These are some of the most amazing local practitioners and business owners I respect, refer my clients to and work with.

1) Katja Heino- Author and Chef
savorylotus.com

2) Jessica Jacobsen- Owner/Chef & Jennifer Foege- Owner/Chef.
Pharm: Food for Thought
pharmfoodforthought.com
missjessicamarie@gmail.com

3) Annie Osborn, L.Ac., Naturopathic Practitioner Rejuvenation Clinic of Sonoma County
AnniesNaturalMedicine.com

4) Emily J. Zeinal, D.C.
Vibrant Life Chiropractic
& Family Wellness Center
vibrantlifechiropractic.net

5) Breast Thermography Center of Sonoma County
Renee and Jen
707-655-5880
thermography-sc.com

6) Erin Prucha, L.Ac, MSOM- Acupuncture/Chinese Herbal Medicine
Specializes in Women's health
AcupunctureSantaRosa.org

7) Dr Sunjya Schweig- California Center for Functional Medicine (CCFM).
ccfmed.com

8) Soul Shine Family Chiropractic-Dr. Bria Iacini, D.C. & Dr. Matthew Mutch, D.C.
soulshinechiro.com
707-525-9950

9) Dr. Shailee Mashruwala- Dr. Rob Oliver Pediatric Dentistry
lifeofsmiles.com

10) Jeanie Gartin- Yoga, Pilates and Photography
jeanieyoga.com

11) Joshua Margolis- Acupuncture and Manual Medicine
farmacopia.net

12) Lily Mazarella- Owner at Farmacopia- Herbalist, CNC
farmacopia.net

13) Jennifer Monin, L.Ac, M.S –Acupuncture/Herbal Medicine
Specializes in Women's health/Pediatrics
www.jennifermonin.com

14) Heather Ashton Black- Mixed Greens Preschool
mixedgreenspreschool.com

15) Ian McCullough-Sebastopol Family Acupuncture
sebastopolfamilyacupuncture.com

16) Michael Rice DDS & Lara Rice DSS- Family Dentistry
santarosadental.com

17) Dawn Dolan- Certified Acupoint Nutritional Testing
rejuvandwellbeing.com

18) Trish Pettitt- facials, reiki, massage & herbal skincare
skinaddictionspa.com

19) Ramona Wilmarth- Hair Artist at Sparrow Hair Co.
707- 541-6096

20) Shelby Neubauer- Owner Sparrow Hair Co.
707-541-6096
Instagram: Sparrow_hair_co

21) Alanna Wargula, DPM- Family Podiatry
parkviewpodiatry.com

22) Anna Joyce, Ph.D, MFT- Nutritional Phycology, EMDR, EFT &
Energy Psycology
707-569-8299
annajoyce11@hotmail.com

23) Judy Fiermonte, MFT-Child and Family Therapist
707-528-1097
judyfiermonte@comcast.net

24) Dr. Lois Johnson- Integrative Holistic Medicine
Hill Park Medical Center
hillparkmedicalcenter.com

25) Dr. Faye Lundergan- Pediatrician
drfayepediatrics.com
Dr. Lundergan was mentored by Dr. Alan R. Greene
Author of *Feeding Baby Green* - drgreene.com

26) Dr. Eileen Roberts Ph.D- Psychologist/ Neurofeedback -
Kids/adults
eileenrobertsphd.com

27) Rosemira Organics- Sebastopol Organic skincare
rosemira.com

28) Trina Palomarez- Clinical Herbalist & Certified Nutrition
Consultant
farmacopia.net
trinapalomarez.com

29) Dr. Michael Arata- Autonomic Nervous System Specialist
autonomicspecialists.com or aratamedical.com

30) Laguna Farms- Sebastopol Local Farm/CSA
lagunafarm.com

31) Julie Inman- Rainbow Bridge Montessori Preschool
rainbowbridgemontessori.com

32) Gena Price- Kids In the Country Early Learning Program/Yoga
Instructor
707-953-8829

National Resources Made Simple!

These are some of my favorite books, magazines, websites & blogs from all over the globe! Google the authors for their great websites.

Books
Digestive Wellness for Children by Elizabeth Lipski, PhD, CCN, CNS, LDN

Digestive Wellness by Elizabeth Lipski, PhD, CCN, CNS, LDN

Nurture My Heart A Nurtured Heart Approach Handbook by Catherine Stafford, LCSW

The Hormone Cure by Dr. Sara Gottfried

Mind Over Medicine by Dr. Lissa Rankin

Naturally Healthy Babies and Children by Aviva Jill Romm

Clean Food by Terry Walters- Cookbook

Clean Start by Terry Walters- Cookbook

Crazy Sexy Diet By Kris Carr- Vegetarian cookbook

Crazy Sexy Juice by Kriss Carr

Paleo Cooking from Elana's Pantry by Elana Amsterdam

The Blood Sugar Solution Cookbook by Dr. Mark Hyman

21 Day Sugar Detox by Diane Sanfilippo

Nourishing Connections Cookbook by Cathryn Couch & JoEllen DeNicola

Magazines and Websites

Paleo Magazine- Paleomagonline.com

Living Without- Livingwithout.com: Gluten- and Dairy-Free

Cooking with your family and friends can create wonderful and lasting connections.
Enjoy!

The Nourishment Made Simple Pantry

Here is a simple grocery list to keep on hand making cooking and meal prep as SIMPLE as possible! These are just a few of my necessary staples:

Flours:
Almond flour, coconut flour and rice flour

Oils:
Coconut oil, olive oil, grapeseed oil

Nuts and Seeds
Chia seeds, flax seeds, almonds, nut butters and pumpkin seeds

Canned Foods- BPA-free brands only!
Coconut milk, organic stewed tomatoes and beans

Dairy items:
Organic eggs, kefir, grass-fed butter and organic butter, ghee

ALL Veggies and Fruits- Rainbow on your plate!
Join a local CSA – www.lagunafarm.com

Other: Vanilla, raw cacao powder, honey, coconut palm sugar, flax meal, Himalayan salt, pepper, cumin, red pepper flakes, turmeric, cinnamon, cardamom, apple cider vinegar, chicken broth, coconut flakes, frozen berries, beans in bulk and oats, maple syrup

Kitchen Equipment and Supplies:
High-speed blender - Blendtec or Vitamix
Mini-muffin pan/food processor
Juicer: Breville Compact Juicer – easy to clean and affordable
Parchment paper

Index

Nourishment Made Simple Plate
Eat a Rainbow on your plate Everyday!

Be nourished and be well the Simple way!

With Love, Amy Hudgens

Made in the USA
San Bernardino, CA
27 April 2018